The Dutch, I Presume?

Icons of the Netherlands

Martijn de Rooi
Jurjen Drenth & friends

N&L Publishing

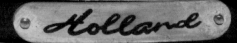

colophon

The Dutch, I presume?
Published by N&L Publishing **Produced by** Dutch Publishers
Concept Allard de Rooi **Text** Martijn de Rooi
Photography Jurjen Drenth, Frans Lemmens, Hein Hage & friends*
Design Maarten van der Kroft **Studio photography** Arthur van der Laan, OXBird.nl
Production and photo editing Jeff Zimberlin, Arend-Jan de Vos, Wendy Meijerink
Translation Tekom Vertalers, Hoofddorp (info@tekom.nl)
Printing Scholma Druk, Bedum (www.scholma.nl) **Thanks to** Kyra Peek

ISBN 90-8541-012-6
Third printing June 2006

Trade distribution Nilsson & Lamm BV, P.O. Box 195, 1380 AD Weesp,
the Netherlands. Telephone: 0294 494 949. E-mail: info@nilsson-lamm.nl.

Dutch Publishers and **Dutch Image** are registered trade names of **The Ad Agency**,
P.O. Box 340, 2400 AH Alphen aan den Rijn, the Netherlands. Telephone: 0172 449 333,
Fax: 0172 495 846. Internet: www.theadagency.nl. E-mail: info@theadagency.nl.

* **Friends are** Allard de Rooi, Arend-Jan de Vos, Arthur van der Laan,
Femke Diets, Hetty van Oijen, Maarten van der Kroft, Martijn de Rooi,
Polle Aubert, Wendy Meijerink and Wilbert Collet.

All photos in this book are provided by Dutch Image.
t: 0172 449 330 i: **www.dutchimage.nl** e: info@dutchimage.nl

**Also available
from N&L Publishing**

Dutch Delight
Typical Dutch Food
ISBN 90-8541-011-8

The Rembrandt Guide
Travelling the world of
the master
ISBN 90-8541-021-5

contents:

👍 **Facts** More than a quarter of the Netherlands lies below sea level • The lowest point in the Netherlands is also the lowest point in Europe and is almost seven metres below sea level • The highest point, the Vaalserberg, is a dizzying 321 metres high • The Netherlands is 'as flat as a pancake'

👎 **Myths** The Dutch have webbed feet, or in any case, they always have wet feet • Tourists always need wellington boots

01

below sea level

MORE THAN A QUARTER OF THE NETHERLANDS LIES BELOW SEA LEVEL, A CAUSE FOR ALARM FOR MANY FOREIGNERS.

see also 📄 **06** water 📄 **10** polders 📄 **36** orderliness

The Low Countries by the Sea

There aren't many countries with such an appropriate name as the Netherlands. The country is unusually low and more than a quarter of its surface is actually below sea level. This fact is as fascinating as it is alarming for foreigners, who are amazed about a country that is 'as flat as a pancake'.

'Do you always have wet feet?'
'Do I need my wellington boots when I come to the Netherlands?'
'Do you all have webbed feet?'
The Dutch have to face the most amazing questions. That's what you get when your country is known above all else as a mysterious and damp place, with some parts of it even below sea level.
The fact that it is so low is an enigma that causes many a foreigner to frown with concern. Land below sea level - what does that look like? Most people imagine the Netherlands as a sunken and soggy meadow. They're in for a surprise when arriving at Schiphol, because although the airport is 4.5 metres below sea level, it is perfectly dry. It is only the name that serves as a reminder of the time that this was the location of a notorious bay with its own ships' graveyard ('ships' hole').

That the Netherlands is low-lying is clear from its unusually appropriate name. Even in the late Middle Ages, the area was known as the Netherlands and the much-used 'Low Countries' also dates from that time. The names are most fitting for the west of the country. A large part of this area, some 27 per cent of the whole country, is below sea level. The lowest point (6.74 metres below sea level) is at Nieuwerkerk aan den IJssel, a small town north-east of Rotterdam. It is also the lowest point in Europe. Without the protection of dunes and dykes, Nieuwerkerk would be permanently submerged, to a depth of almost seven metres. The boundary between the 'low' and 'high' Netherlands zigzags capriciously across the country. In 2004 large signs were positioned at 27 motorway parking areas, indicating the location of the boundary. But depths and altitude in the Netherlands are not set in stone. They are constantly changing thanks to the rising sea level, the steadily sinking west of the country and the gradual rising of the land in the east. The Dutch themselves, ever immersed in the task of keeping the land under control, also play their part in this process. The Prins Alexanderpolder near Rotterdam is a case in point. For a long time it had a depth of seven metres below sea level, and so was the proud bearer of the 'lowest point in the Netherlands' title. In 1995, though, it appeared that they had, for building purposes, elevated the ground so much that the polder was forced to relinquish its coveted record and make do with a modest 6.25 metres below sea level.

East of the boundary the land rises gradually, but compared with most other countries the differences in altitude are minimal. The Netherlands is flat, 'as flat as a pancake', as the Dutch say, referring to the well-known local culinary speciality. The highest point is near Vaals, a small town in the extreme south-east of the country, on the border with Belgium and Germany. The so-called Drielandenpunt – the place where the three countries meet – reaches a height of 321 metres, a hill that only in the Netherlands could be described as a 'mountain'. ▪

> **Tourists arriving at Schiphol airport are in for a surprise, because although it is 4.5 metres below sea level, it is perfectly dry.**

01 The village of Winssen **05** Hilly country near the Drielandenpunt, the highest point of the Netherlands **06** High water near Wilp

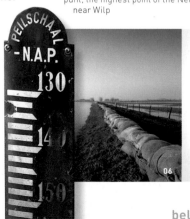

Facts One fifth of the Netherlands consists of water • Twenty per cent of the country has been reclaimed from the water • Without protection two-thirds of the Netherlands would frequently be flooded • The Dutch are the world champions in water management • The storm surge barrier in the Nieuwe Waterweg is called the 'eighth wonder of the world' • Rotterdam is the second largest port in the world • The Amsterdam Defence Line consisting of waterworks and forts is included on the World Heritage List

01

water

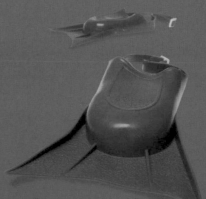

**'GOD CREATED THE WORLD,
BUT THE DUTCH CREATED THE NETHERLANDS'.**

Friend and foe

Water and the Netherlands are inextricably bound together. Without the dunes, dykes and other flood barriers, two-thirds of the country would frequently be flooded. Circumstances have therefore compelled the people of the Netherlands to become world champions in water management. However, the water has also brought prosperity and is one of the great attractions of the Low Countries.

01 The beach and the storm surge barrier in the Oosterschelde near Burg-Haamstede 02 Water tower near Goes 03 The Afsluitdijk at Den Oever 04 Farmer in Giethoorn

The eternal battle against the water is the price paid by the Dutch for the low lie of their country. At high water, two-thirds of the country would be inundated on a regular basis. In order to survive in this wet marshland, the Dutch people have been forced to become hydraulic engineers.

Around 500 BC the Frisians were the first to take measures against the water. They built their villages on artificial mounds up to fifteen metres high, known as terps or wierds. The first dykes were constructed in the year 1000 or thereabouts, and four hundred years later the Dutch learned how to reclaim large areas of land with the aid of that wonder of technology: the windmill. The introduction of the steam-driven pumping station around 1800 enabled them to perfect the art.

Major catastrophes, such as the St Elizabeth Flood that in 1421 struck the south-west of the Netherlands and its many islands, played an important role in this development. In 1916 serious flooding in the province of Noord-Holland formed the incentive for the construction of the Afsluitdijk (Enclosing Dyke), which is over thirty kilometres long and was completed in 1932. With the creation of this dyke, the Zuider Sea, a large bay that had been hollowed out by the sea, was downgraded to an inland lake, part of which was subsequently drained.

In 1953 a storm surge in the south-west of the Netherlands took the lives of almost two thousand people. The people of the Netherlands struck back by creating an extensive complex of dykes and dams that linked the islands and reduced the coastline of the North Sea from 1080 to 380 kilometres. The crowning glory of these so-called Deltaworks is the storm surge barrier in the Nieuwe Waterweg, which was completed in 1997 and is known as the 'eighth wonder of the world'.

The eternal battle against the water has been a decisive factor in making the Netherlands what it is today and has left its mark on almost every part of the Dutch landscape. Twenty per cent of the country consists of land that has been reclaimed from the water, and the dunes, dykes and other waterworks are omnipresent. The Dutch are not held back by any sense of false modesty when reflecting on their remarkable achievements in this respect. A common saying is, 'God created the world, but the Dutch created the Netherlands'.

Dutch know-how in this field commands respect far beyond the national boundaries. The Dutch are considered to be the world champions in water management. Major Dutch companies like Volker Stevin, Smit International and Mammoet, partly responsible for the salvage of the Russian nuclear submarine *Kursk*, are the first in line if something has to be salvaged, dredged or constructed in foreign waters. Whether this concerns drainage, land reclamation, bridge building or harbour construction, Dutch engineers belong to the best in all fields.

The Dutch have been compelled to become world champions in water management.

However, the water is not just an antagonist. It can be very useful, and the people of the Netherlands know how to exploit the many opportunities it offers. Over the centuries the Netherlands has played a leading role in shipping, shipbuilding and overseas trade. The country owed and still owes much of its prosperity to these sectors. Rotterdam is the second largest port in the world after Shanghai, and Dutch ships play an important role in the European inland shipping sector. Within the country itself, water transport is still very common, with even livestock being transported by boat in rural areas. There is also a substantial fishing fleet consisting of around five hundred ships and a total of 2500 crew members, who are responsible for landing the popular Dutch delicacy of herring.

The omnipresent water is one of the great attractions of the Netherlands. One fifth of the country consists of water, and it is very difficult to find a place that does not have a view of a lake, pool, river, canal, waterway, moat, ditch or harbour. The main tourist attractions are the coastline with its wide sandy beaches and magnificent dunes, the cities with their picturesque canals, and the numerous lakes and pools – in particular the famous Frisian lakes. Another unique feature is the Wadden Sea, located between the northern coast and the Wadden Islands. This is an expansive area of natural beauty that falls dry at low tide, attracting adventurous ramblers.

In times of great need, the people of the Netherlands even used the water as an ally. They retreated behind the Hollandse Waterlinie (Holland Waterline), a broad strip of land that could be flooded and was protected by a line of forts. Water also played an important role in defending cities. The unique Stelling van Amsterdam (Amsterdam Defence Line), which is 135 kilometres long and consists of forts, waterworks and sections of land that could be flooded, is included on the UNESCO World Heritage List.

The modern Defence Line, the impressive Deltaworks, gives the population a sense of security. However, some caution is still required in the Netherlands of the twenty-first century. Recently overflowing rivers and subsiding dykes necessitated the evacuation of entire villages. In such cases there is a common call for the victims to be compensated, and prominent people put on their wellingtons and rush to the scene of the disaster to show their support. Even the Queen has been known to show up if the disaster is serious enough. *Luctor et emergo* (I struggle and overcome) is not only the motto in the coat of arms of the province of Zeeland, it is the motto of the Netherlands as a whole when the traditional foe threatens the country. ∎

07 The Zeeland bridge over the Oosterschelde **09** Pollard willows along the Waal near Afferden **12** The storm surge barrier in the Oosterschelde **15** The Hef bridge in Rotterdam **16** Nieuwerkerk, during the storm surge of 1953 and at present **17** The Wadden Sea at low tide **18** By ferry to the church on a Sunday, Nederhemert **19** Shipmaster docking at Grevelinge

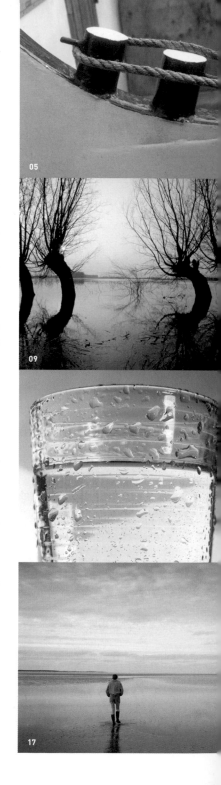

Facts Over sixty percent of the Netherlands is made up of polders • The IJsselmeerpolders are the biggest polders in the world • Two polders and a steam-powered pumping station, symbols of man's battle against the sea, are on the UNESCO World Heritage List • The Dutch word 'polder' has entered countless languages, from Czech to Japanese

Myths All polders are below sea level • The polder model is a scale model of a polder

01

polders

THE IJSSELMEERPOLDERS ARE THE BIGGEST POLDERS IN THE WORLD, A POTENT SYMBOL OF THE DUTCH CONVICTION OF THE 'MALLEABILITY' OF LANDSCAPE AND SOCIETY.

see also ☐ 04 below sea level ☐ 06 water ☐ 36 orderliness ☐ 46 windmills

New land

Vast, green, orderly planes blanketed by never-ending skies: the polder is the trademark symbol of the Dutch landscape. Polders make up sixty percent of the landmass of the Netherlands. The IJsselmeer-polders are the biggest in the world and form the 'new land', a chessboard-like landscape that has been planned down to the very last detail.

The Netherlands is studded with polders, parcels of land surrounded by dykes with artificially regulated water levels. There are thousands upon thousands of polders, making up sixty percent of the Netherlands. The majority of polders have been created by reclaiming land from lakes and ponds below sea level. We can also distinguish peat and sea polders: drained peat meadows, usually at or just below sea level, and embanked sections of sea above sea level.

The first, rather modestly-sized polders were constructed by the Frisians in the north of the country in the 12th or 13th century. Although they were able to drain parcels of land within the dykes, they did not have the required technology to tackle large-scale projects. That technology arrived in the 14th century in the form of the windmill. It became possible to drain huge lakes using inter-connected windmills. The hydraulic engineer and pioneering windmill builder Jan Adriaensz Leeghwater created a stir in the 17th century by transforming multiple lakes into polders using dozens of windmills. His first big success came in 1612 with the draining of the Beemstermeer [Beemster Lake] to the north of Amsterdam. De Beemster, the oldest area of reclaimed land in the Netherlands, is renowned for its beautiful, carefully parcelled landscape, and has rightly been included on the UNESCO World Heritage List.

More large-scale drainage projects followed with the introduction of the steam-powered pumping station, around 1800. Before the advent of electric pumping stations, the Netherlands boasted over seven hundred steam-powered pumping stations. The Woudagemaal in Lemmer, a giant industrial monument, is one of the few remaining pumping stations. It is the biggest steam-powered pumping station in the world and is included on the World Heritage List.

Polder model and Dutch disease

The battle against the sea has not only transformed the Dutch landscape, but also strongly influenced the political and administrative culture of the country. To keep your head above water in the Low Countries, consultation and teamwork are essential. During the Middle Ages, this necessity led to the creation of democratic organisations. Water boards, charged with overseeing water management and water defence projects, would only conclude practical compromises after all the involved parties had had their say. This solidified the reputation of the Dutch as sober mediators.

This consultative approach to reaching a consensus gradually became a general feature of political and administrative life in the Netherlands, and has become known as the 'polder model' even outside the Netherlands. The main focus of international attention was on the regular consultations between the government, trade unions and employers' organisations, designed to enable economically sound progress. For a while, the polder model was held up as a shining example of Dutch achievements: There was even an intensive flurry of polder tourism: overseas politicians travelled to the Netherlands to sample this successful formula. However, as soon as economic growth turned to economic stagnation, this jubilation turned to criticism. The decision-making process was at best 'treacly', the Dutch mockingly referred to themselves as world champions in organising meetings, a far from flattering title, a veiled reference to the lack of decisiveness. The polder model was 'much ado about nothing', to coin an apt phrase. Other countries have been equally critical. This once highly praised consultation structure has become known as 'the Dutch disease'.

01 Polder road near Haastrecht 02 The Binnenhof in The Hague, where both Chambers of Parliament are located

The Noordoostpolder represents a perfect geometric pattern, crafted at the drawing table down to the nearest millimetre.

The undisputed pinnacle of Dutch 'poldering' excellence however is the so-called Zuider Sea project. It was the initiative of the hydraulic engineer and Minister of Transport, Public Works and Water Management Cornelis Lely. The construction of the Afsluitdijk (Enclosing Dyke) constituted the first phase of this immense project, which transformed the dangerous Zuider Sea into an inner lake, the IJssel Lake. This became the home of the biggest polders in the world:

the Noordoostpolder (completed in 1942), Oostelijk Flevoland (1957) and Zuidelijk Flevoland (1968). Together, they form the 'new land', a potent symbol of the Dutch conviction of the 'malleability' of landscape and society. The Noordoostpolder in particular is unrivalled in its planning detail. From the air, this polder represents a perfect geometric pattern, crafted at the drawing table down to the last millimetre.
At the heart of this mathematic precision is a special

monument: the former island of Schokland. In the past, this small, low-lying island was a plaything for the savage Zuider Sea. The population fought a long yet futile battle against the sea, and the remaining seven hundred islanders were ordered to leave their homes in 1859. Since 1942, Schokland has been at the heart of the polder. In 1995, it became the first Dutch monument to be included on the World Heritage List as a symbol of man's constant battle against the sea. The triumphs of Lely were held in such high regard that in the 'new land' a town was named after him. But Almere is possibly even more famous than Lelystad.

It is the youngest city of the Netherlands. Renowned for its modern architecture, Almere is expected to be home to 215 thousant people by 2010, making it the fifth largest municipality of the Netherlands. ■

03 The Zuider Sea Museum in Enkhuizen **04** Pumping station De Block in Almere **05** Old pumping station in Medemblik **07** Typical chessboard-like polder landscape **08** Pumping station Cruquius near Haarlem **11 & 13** Almere **12** The former port of the former island of Schokland **15** Polder landscape in Zuidelijk Flevoland

Facts Hans Brinker became world famous as the hero of a popular book • There are statues of Hans in Spaarndam and Harlingen
Myths Hans really existed • He prevented a flood by sticking his finger into a hole in a dyke

Hans Brinker

THE AMERICANS CAN'T GET ENOUGH OF HANS BRINKER, THE INCARNATION OF THE ETERNAL STRUGGLE OF THE TINY NETHERLANDS AGAINST THE MIGHTY SEA.

see also 📖 04 below sea level 📖 06 water 📖 10 polders 📖 134 ice-skating

World famous, just not in the Netherlands

Hans Brinker is one of the world's most famous Dutch people, but he is virtually unknown in the Netherlands. And what the Dutch think they know about him is wrong.

Hans Brinker: what name could possibly sound more Dutch? He gained eternal fame by sticking a finger into a hole in a dyke, thus saving the country from a disastrous flood. He was only eight, this lad from Spaarndam, and he had to wait hours for help at night, chilled to the bone: a truly heroic deed. No surprise then that the Dutch put up a statue to him – two, in fact, in Spaarndam and in Harlingen.

But ask a random Dutch person about the boy and there's a good chance that the reply will be 'Who? A hero? Statues?' Now, the Dutch are never ones to put their heroic compatriots on a pedestal without a good reason, but they're overdoing it a bit with Brinker: despite all the tributes, most have no idea who he was. At most, one or two can come up with a vague memory: 'Wasn't that the kid with the finger?'

Outside the Netherlands, things are much different: his heroic deed is appreciated. The Americans in particular are taken with Hans, the incarnation of the struggle of the tiny Netherlands against the mighty sea. It's a story they can't get enough of, so much so that there was even a book about Hans.

Hans Brinker or The Silver Skates was the title, and it was written around 1865 by Mary Mapes Dodge. This writer of children's books had never visited the Netherlands but wanted nonetheless to acquaint her audience with the amiable little country beside the North Sea. Her book sketches a romantic, American view of the Netherlands – a country full of windmills, water, ice and skates. At its core are the adventures of Hans, who seeks to lighten the sorry existence of his family by taking part in a skating competition, in the hope of winning a pair of silver skates.

Like everything in the book, little Hans was the product of the writer's imagination. Hans Brinker never existed, never mind the part about singlehandedly sealing a leaky dyke, which in the story is not even Hans' doing but that of another boy. Yet the book appealed to imaginations everywhere and was pub-lished in translation in many countries. In both the United States and Japan seven million copies were sold. Hans Brinker became world famous as 'the boy with his finger in the dyke'.

The book was also published in the Netherlands but was much less popular there. In the meantime, though, the first pilgrims from abroad began to ar-rive in Spaarndam, seeking real life reminders of the young hero. The tourist office had little choice but to put up a statue of him, where tourists now explain who Hans Brinker was to surprised locals. ∎

In the meantime, the first pilgrims from abroad began to arrive in Spaarndam, seeking real life reminders of the young hero.

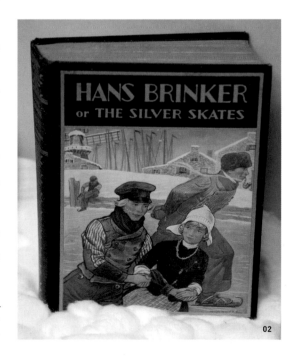

01 & 02 Farmers, small towns, dykes, lots of water and skaters: the book *Hans Brinker or The Silver Skates* sketches a romantic view of life in the Netherlands

Facts Amsterdam has the largest canal system in the world and the most bridges of any European city • Over three million tourists step aboard an Amsterdam canal boat each year • The Utrecht canals with their characteristic wharves are unique in the world • Many canals were drained once they fell into disuse • A growing number of municipalities want to excavate the drained canals

Myths Canals are for throwing bikes into and are ideal for sobering up drunk café patrons

01

canals

CANALS ARE OFTEN USED AS PUBLIC TRASHCANS, BUT THANKS TO THE MONUMENTAL BUILDINGS AND HISTORIC BRIDGES THEY HAVE BECOME A CROWD PULLER IN THEIR OWN RIGHT.

see also 42 architecture 96 VOC 118 Amsterdam

From waterway to historic attraction

Canals are one of the biggest attractions the Netherlands has to offer. With their ancient bridges, houses and narrow streets, they lend an historic charm to towns and cities. The canals traditionally served as waterways and defence works. Once they had fallen into disuse, many canals were drained. A number of municipalities have regretted this step, and are drawing up plans to excavate the drained canals.

The Netherlands has countless cities with canals, many of which are particularly charming and well worth a visit. The most special canals however can be found in Amsterdam. Canals are a potent symbol of the capital and the main theme of many a *Mokum* tearjerker. Amsterdam boasts the most extensive canal system in the world. The city has approximately 160 canals, totalling over one hundred kilometres in length. The 'canal belt' of the 'Golden' 17th century, when Amsterdam was the trade capital of the world, has become a world-famous attraction. To accommodate the explosive population growth, three parallel main canals were constructed in 1613 outside the walls of the medieval city. Along these canals, the powerful merchants built their beautiful homes.

The three canals became the exclusive preserve of the ruling classes. To a certain degree, they still are. The term 'canal belt' has a dubious connotation, referring to the self-appointed intellectual and cultural *corps d'elite*, whose opinions are not always understood by those residing outside the belt.

Although the Amsterdam canals are often used as public trashcans – the dumping of disused bikes is a particularly popular pastime – they have retained much of their historic charm. The best way to enjoy these canals is of course from the comfort of a boat. Over three million tourists a year climb aboard the canal boats for a tour around the historic open-air museum that is the Amsterdam city centre. The city has about eight thousand monuments, including countless merchant houses, warehouses and of course bridges. Amsterdam has over 1500 bridges, more than any other European city. The countless houseboats are an equally imposing feature of the capital. There are several hundred in the inner city alone, and no fewer than 2400 throughout the entire city.

As mentioned above, Amsterdam is not the only Dutch city to boast an illustrious network of canals.

> Some canals were open sewerage systems and produced such a ghastly smell that council officials did not need a detailed zoning plan to vote in favour of immediate draining.

01 Amsterdam, intersection of the Keizersgracht and Leidsegracht
03 Amersfoort **04** 'Boat musician' Reinier Sijpkens giving a concert in an Amsterdam canal

Which other cities are worth a mention? Leiden, with its Rapenburg, is particularly impressive, as are the charming canals of Utrecht, with their characteristic, low-level quays. These wharves are connected to the canalside houses via deep, underground boat-yard cellars, enabling easy loading and unloading of commodities. The quays were constructed between 1300 and 1500 and are unique in the world. With their eating houses, cafés and terraces, the boatyard cellars and wharves are an important feature of Utrecht nightlife. Many a café dweller has returned home soaked after a 'night on the town'. ■

05 Characteristic canalside houses at the Voldersgracht, Delft
06 & 11 Pedal boats in the canals of Utrecht, well-known for their unique wharves 08 Flower stall at the Prinsengracht, Amsterdam
09 The 17th century Magere Brug in Amsterdam, spanning the Amstel 10 Former VOC warehouse in Amsterdam

The canal revival

In numerous Dutch cities, canals and even harbours were drained once they had fallen into disuse. They made way for roads, houses or shops, or, in their capacity as open sewerage systems, produced such a ghastly smell that council officials did not need a detailed zoning plan to vote in favour of immediate draining. A growing number of cities are beginning to realise that this decision has contributed to the erosion of the country's cultural-historic heritage, and are drawing up plans to revive the old waterworks. One example is the fortified town of Heusden, where the drained harbour has been excavated.

The weather is an inexhaustible topic of conversation • The Netherlands has four seasons that differ considerably • Rainfall averages out at almost ninety minutes a day • Dutch people hate rain but love snow • The weather forecast for the long term is more rain and less snow
In the Netherlands it rains for 366 days a year

climate

THE FIRST HOT SUMMER DAY IS HAILED WITH JOY AND ENDS WITH SUNBURN AND A FITFUL SLEEP.

see also 📄 24 beaches 📄 134 ice-skating

Sluggish winters and the wind chill factor

The Netherlands is a land of water. The people of the Netherlands have wet feet and rain-sodden heads, according to one jocular saying. Many people, including the Dutch themselves, are convinced that it is always raining in this watery country, but actually the Dutch climate is not quite as bad as people tend to think. In any case, it is a popular topic of conversation, which can be useful if bad weather forces you to stay indoors.

The Dutch and the weather have a strange relationship. The weather is a never-ending source of inspiration for starting up or continuing a conversation. When the sun shines, we hear 'Lovely weather, isn't it?', but when the rain drowns everything in sight, this changes to 'What dreadful weather!'.
The Dutch seem to be obsessed with the weather, and rain is the main focus of this obsession. Perhaps this is not surprising if you consider that cycling in a downpour cannot be much fun.
Before you know it you are soaked, sodden, dripping wet, drenched – and in the Dutch language there are even more terms to describe anything that has to do with water.
Even so, we shouldn't exaggerate. The common notion among foreigners is that it rains in the Netherlands for 366 days a year, and quite a few Dutch people will confirm this, especially when their country is being battered by yet another storm. However, the actual facts tell a different story. According to statistics, rain falls on approximately 190 days a year. This is usually just a small shower. Rainfall exceeding ten millimetres only occurs on about twenty days a year. All in all it rains in the Netherlands for no more than six per cent of the time, which averages out at less than ninety minutes a day.
This six per cent is not divided equally over the four seasons. The chance of needing an umbrella and wellingtons is greatest in autumn and winter, although a severe autumn gale can turn the umbrella into a useless and rather ridiculous piece of equipment.
For the Dutch, autumn is the ideal time to take a breath of fresh air. The best place for doing this is on the beach, and the best beaches of all are on the Wadden Islands. Even if you get soaking wet on your autumn stroll, back in the warm and dry with a cup of steaming cocoa, you feel like an heroic adventurer and you view the enterprise as an invigorating challenge for both mind and body. Incidentally, such heroism is not everyone's cup of tea. Some people prefer to fly a kite in autumn, or walk in the woods and admire the glorious golden leaves and abundant toadstools. Others choose to pass the chilly autumn days in an armchair next to the fire.
The occasional winter storms can be rather dramatic. The cold weather is not a problem, but cold in combination with wind is disastrous.
The meteorologists fall over themselves to explain the concept of the wind chill factor, and cheerfully state that minus five degrees Celsius feels like minus twenty. These are the worst conditions of all for taking a soaking.

Snow is an intrinsic part of Dutch winters. The white blanket may cause chaos on the roads, but it also creates beautiful landscapes.

01 Spring in Tricht 02 Summer near Goudriaan 03 Autumn near Doorn 04 Winter in Heesbeen

However, a snowfall is a completely different kettle of fish. The Dutch see the snow as an intrinsic part of Dutch winters. The white blanket may cause chaos on the roads, but it also creates beautiful landscapes – and what could be more fun than throwing snowballs and making a snowman? Snow generates a cosy atmosphere. More importantly, the ice-skates can be dug out and dusted off. Dutch people look forward to ice-skating all year long. Wind and snow do not pose an obstacle to skating; on the contrary, they turn a long skating trip into a challenge, similar to getting soaking wet on an autumn stroll. A winter without snow and frost is not a proper winter, it is a *kwakkelwinter* or sluggish winter. Unfortunately the chance of sluggish winters is apparently increasing because of the greenhouse effect, which to make matters worse will also produce more rain.

The meteorologists cheerfully state that minus five degrees Celsius feels like minus twenty.

After a sluggish winter, the greater is the relief when the dark days are finally blown away by spring skies like those depicted in famous Dutch paintings. Trees develop leaves, plants begin to sprout, the countryside turns green and the heavy showers die down. During spring everyone begins to look forward to a hot summer. The first hot day is hailed with joy, and ends with sunburn and a fitful sleep. When the weather gets really hot, the entire population of the Netherlands seems to seek cooling in the North Sea. They get soaking wet here, too, but as long as it is not from the rain, nobody seems to mind. ■

09 Tanning on a sunbed **15** Autumn in the scenic area called Planken Wambuis near Ede **16** Springtime near Buurmalsen

15

16

01 02 03 04 05

beaches

THE DUTCH COASTLINE IS RENOWNED FOR ITS BEAUTIFUL WIDE SANDY BEACHES, BORDERED BY EQUALLY BEAUTIFUL SAND DUNES.

Facts The 380-kilometre long Dutch coastline is graced by wide, white sandy beaches • Zandvoort and Scheveningen are particularly popular seaside resorts • Beaches can also be found along many lakes and ponds • A growing number of cities are building temporary beaches during the summer months, some complete with palm trees

Myths The Netherlands cuts a sorry figure as a beach destination

see also 20 climate

The Netherlands' white flank

The Dutch coastline, with its beautiful white sandy beaches, is a real crowd puller. Seaside resorts such as Zandvoort and Scheveningen are renowned for their vibrant beaches on hot summer days. Outside these areas, there is ample opportunity to savour the sand, sea and sun in peace and quiet. It is now even possible to sunbathe under urban palm trees!

The Netherlands has a universal reputation as a cold and rain-swept country. It is not exactly renowned for its sun-kissed beaches. It may therefore come as a surprise to find that the country provides ample temptation for the true beach lover. The 380-kilometre coastline is jammed packed with jaw-droppingly beautiful wide sandy beaches, bordered by equally impressive high dunes, perfect flood defences.
Dutch beaches are a tourist attraction in their own right. A brisk walk along the beach is a popular Dutch pastime: strolling along fierce breakers, stopping only to admire a beautiful seashell or to eat herring at a fish cart, is the perfect way to 'recharge the batteries'.

Zandvoort and Scheveningen are ideal locations for a night on the town after a day at the beach.

During the summer, the Dutch visit the coast en-masse for a brief respite from the heat. On the heavily visited beaches of the popular seaside resorts of Zandvoort and Scheveningen it becomes apparent just how incredibly densely poplated the Netherlands is. But life at a crowded beach is far from stressful: children building sandcastles while their parents leaf through a book, youngsters parading along the floodmark, dogs playing around in the breakers, people eating copious amounts of ice cream in the beach tents. Partygoers are also catered for, with live bands in the festive party tents and parties on the beach. Zandvoort and Scheveningen are ideal locations for a night on the town after a day at the beach. A more relaxed ambience is provided by seaside resorts such as Bloemendaal, Noordwijk, Egmond and Katwijk, and along the beautiful beaches of the Wadden Islands.

Dutch seaside resorts are also a popular attraction for overseas visitors. The all-pervading *Zimmer frei* signs reveal immediately that the majority of these overseas visitors are German. Sixty years on from the Second World War, and the relationship between the Dutch and their eastern neighbours is still somewhat strained. The Germans are admittedly addressed politely and in their own language, but referred to rather unflatteringly as *Moffen*, a term synonymous with loud-mouthed arrogance. The resentment over the war years has spilled over to the younger generation. Dutch teenagers love to poke fun at the perceived German custom of digging big holes along the beach, while a Dutch footballing victory over the Germans is celebrated with as much panache as a winning lottery ticket.
To enjoy the beach, you do not necessarily need to drive to the coast. Small beaches straddle the lakes and ponds of the country, and a growing number of cities are building beaches along their rivers or canals during the summer, complete with sun lounges, parasols and the occasional palm tree. Urban beaches are a peaceful sanctuary for urban sun worshippers. The only thing missing is the calm, peaceful rustling of the waves. ■

05 Beach fun at Zoutelande 06 Tanning at the beach of the famous seaside resort of Zandvoort

01

people

THE DUTCH POPULATION IS STRONGLY MULTICULTURAL. MOST DUTCH PEOPLE HAVE ANCESTORS WHO CAME TO THE LOW COUNTRIES AS IMMIGRANTS, OFTEN CENTURIES AGO.

see also 📄 34 language 📄 36 orderliness 📄 124 tolerance

The Dutch, I presume?

The Netherlands is a densely populated, multicultural and predominantly secular country full of friendly people who would mostly like to be as normal as possible. A brief introduction to the Netherlands. Or is it Holland?

In early 2005, the Netherlands had 16.3 million inhabitants. At an average of 480 people per square kilometre, it is not only the most densely populated country in Europe, but also one of the most densely populated in the world. A large part of the population live in what is called the Randstad, a huge agglomeration in the west of the country that includes the four major cities of Amsterdam (715 thousand inhabitants), Rotterdam (600 thousand), The Hague (480 thousand) and Utrecht (280 thousand).

The Dutch population is strongly multicultural. Most Dutch people have ancestors who came to the Low Countries as immigrants, often centuries ago. At present, a fifth of the population is considered foreign, most of them of non-Western origin and residing in the major cities.

The largest foreign group, numbering about 400 thousand, consists of people from the former colony of the Dutch East Indies and their descendants. Immediately after the Indies declared their independence under the name Indonesia in 1945, 80 thousand Dutch citizens living in the colony, 180 thousand people of mixed Dutch and Indonesian origin and 12.5 thousand Moluccans came to the Netherlands.

Many also came from the former colonies of Surinam and the Netherlands Antilles. Around the time that Surinam was declared independent in 1975, 145 thousand Surinamese, or one third of Surinam's population, emigrated to the Netherlands. The Surinamese community in the Netherlands currently numbers 325 thousand. Another 130 thousand people came from the Netherlands Antilles and Aruba – Caribbean islands that are still part of the Kingdom of the Netherlands.

The Dutch are seen as informal and approachable abroad, as accessible as their flat homeland.

The Netherlands is also home to 352 thousand Turks and 306 thousand Moroccans. Along with a number of smaller groups of people from Mediterranean countries, the first Turks and Moroccans arrived decades ago as 'guest workers'. Most were planning to return home eventually, but in practice this was seldom the case.

The arrival of a large number of people from Muslim countries, combined with rapid secularisation since the 1960s, has dramatically changed the religious

01 The traditional New Year's dive in Scheveningen **03** Celebrating carnival in the south of the country **05** Proudly showing a Koran at a Zaandam mosque

02   03   04   05

Not every Dutch person (Nederlander) is a Hollander, but every Hollander is a citizen of the Netherlands.

landscape of the Netherlands. The majority of Dutch people now have no religious affiliation. Catholics form the largest group of believers, most of them living south of the country's major rivers. Protestants dominate the area to the north. For this reason, the Catholic carnival holiday is exuberantly celebrated in the south but generally considered crass entertainment in the north.

Islam is the country's third-largest religion. There are about one million Muslims and in some communities the Islamic call to prayer is now as familiar a sound as the pealing of church bells.

A striking characteristic of Dutch society is its strongly egalitarian character. Social standing is based more on individual achievement than on origin or birth, and the average Dutch person is somewhat averse to hierarchies and authorities, especially those that act in a high-handed manner. Ostentation and affectation are not popular, the Dutch prefer seriousness and simplicity to pomp and circumstance. 'Acting normally is crazy enough,' as a Dutch saying has it.

The Dutch are also quick to address each other using informal pronouns and by first names. Even in primary education, teachers are often addressed familiarly by their pupils. The Dutch are therefore seen as informal and approachable abroad, as accessible as their flat homeland. They are considered interested and open and are appreciated for their ability to adjust to different customs. ■

Conversely, their openness and directness are sometimes seen as a lack of tact and manners, and foreigners are surprised by their lack of spontaneity regarding meals and visits: these must be arranged in advance. The Dutch are no strangers to spontaneity, but respect for each other's privacy and a deep-rooted need for order in life make diaries a prominent and much-used feature in this densely populated country. ■

30 Children of a miller in Kinderdijk **31** Map showing the former county of Holland (in yellow), the present-day provinces of North and South Holland

Netherlands or Holland?

The co-existence of the names 'Netherlands' and 'Holland' sometimes leads to confusion. Many outsiders believe both to refer to the entire country, but Holland is only the western part - the modern provinces of North and South Holland. In the past, Holland was the foremost of the seven regions that in 1581, on the initiative of Holland, formed the Republic of the Seven United Netherlands, the forerunner of today's Kingdom of the Netherlands. So not every Dutch person (Nederlander) is a Hollander, but every Hollander is indeed a citizen of the Netherlands. The Dutch themselves contribute to the confusion by frequently referring to their country as Holland.

Facts The popularity of the colour orange is related to Oranje, the name of the Dutch royal family • The House of Orange has its roots in what is now Germany • The relationship between Orange and the Netherlands arose in resistance to Spanish dominance in the 16th century • The leader of the resistance, William of Orange, is the 'Father of the Fatherland' • Most Dutch people are fairly indifferent to the monarchy • 'King Football' is more popular

Orange

WHEN THE DUTCH FOOTBALL TEAM PLAYS A MAJOR TOURNAMENT, THE COUNTRY SUCCUMBS TO ORANGE FEVER. ENTIRE NEIGHBOURHOODS ARE DECORATED WITH ORANGE GARLANDS AND FLAGS, AND RESIDENTS WATCH TELEVISION IN THE STREET.

The colour of monarchs and merriment

The Dutch monarchy has mostly folkloric significance. Few cherish the Orange dynasty, but even fewer in the Netherlands want to get rid of the monarchy. Once a year, the country dresses up in orange and the royal family is a source of unity and communal celebration.

On *Koninginnedag*, the Netherlands celebrates the Queen's official birthday. In most towns and villages large markets are held, surrounded by all manner of festivities. Full of good cheer and draped in orange, the Dutch crowd market stalls and terraces, and the party ends in fireworks and, for many, a hefty Orange hangover.

The monarch celebrates modestly, visiting demonstrations of old-fashioned sack races and lace-making. Beatrix (or 'Bea', as she is popularly known) shows her best side, dispensing a friendly word here and there and a smile from time to time. She is considered a little distant, but also serious and involved in her own way.

Crown Prince Willem-Alexander is somewhat more outgoing and closer to the people, especially since his marriage to an Argentine extrovert. He is devoted to Dutch athletes and dedicated to an ultra-Dutch discipline: water management.

The House of Orange, to its benefit, is seen by most Dutch people as relatively 'normal'. In other monarchies, their modest palaces would at best be used for keeping the royal carriages. In many respects the House of Orange is a truly Dutch royal family, although their roots lie in the medieval county of Nassau, which lies in what is now the country's big (and sometimes bad) neighbour, Germany.

The Nassaus had extensive possessions and influence in the regions that would later be known as the Netherlands. The clan also inherited the principality of Orange in the south of France, so that in the mid-1500s, the title 'Prince of Orange', together with the possessions in the Netherlands, ended up with a certain William, nicknamed 'the Silent'. At the time, the Netherlands was an unwilling part of a large Spanish kingdom, and the influential William gradually became the leader of the resistance to the occupation.

It was the start of a connection between the House of Orange and the Netherlands and also the impetus for the creation of an independent Netherlands. Partly on William's initiative, seven regions joined together to resist Spain.

On the Queen's birthday, she visits demonstrations of old-fashioned sack races and lace-making.

02 Magazines on the House of Orange 03 Tin containing orange sprinkles and showing the portrait of the present-day Queen Beatrix 04 The Queen arriving at the Binnenhof in The Hague in the golden coach for the traditional opening of the parliamentary year in September

Flags and pennants

The red-white-and-blue Dutch flag first appeared in the 16th century in the struggle against Spanish dominance. This first flag had orange in its upper bar as a tribute by the insurgents to their leader, William of Orange. This is the source of the slogan *Oranje boven* [Up with Orange]. Blue was the colour of the Nassau clan.

Shortly thereafter, orange was replaced by red for reasons that are unclear. There was bickering over the flag well into the last century: should it be red or orange after all? It remained red-white-and-blue, but on the queen's birthday, an orange pennant is attached to the top of the flagpole. The pennant is absent on all other occasions, although the flag is flown at half-mast on May 4, Remembrance Day. The Netherlands is the only country in the world with such a variety of ways of flying the flag.

BEATRIX – CLAUS

The Spaniards were not amused and sent bounty hunters to capture William. He was murdered in 1584 in Delft and buried in a tomb in the New Church, where all members of the royal family have been buried since. The struggle against Spain ended in 1648 with a victory for the Republic of the Seven United Netherlands, and William of Orange entered the history books as the 'Father of the Fatherland'.

Nonetheless, the Dutch are not fervent royalists today. Most of the population does not want to be rid of the monarchy but does not feel strongly about it either. It's just a part of life and folklore.

The House of Orange causes a small minority to see red, especially because of a fair number of scandals involving the royal family. An unnecessary institution that causes so much trouble and costs a bundle in taxes as well, is not something they are attached to. There is also more principled resistance: a small number of people dismiss the hereditary monarchy as being anti-democratic. There is even some sym-

bolic yapping from a Republican Society from time to time. Opposition to the monarchy is mainly folklore as well.

The average Dutch person is not bothered and faithfully puts on an orange T-shirt on the Queen's birthday. In recent decades, the 'Orange feeling' has spread to other events as well. If the Dutch football team is in a major tournament, the country succumbs to orange fever. Streets and entire neighbourhoods are decorated with orange garlands, flags and ban-

ners, and neighbours watch television together in the street, united in conviviality and unbridled happiness in their orange shirts. It is only on these days that the monarchy is a source of unity, in joint celebrations. ■

05 Picture postcards showing Queen Beatrix and her late husband Claus [above] and Crown Prince Willem-Alexander **06** William of Orange **07** Queen Beatrix on *Koninginnedag* **08** The tomb of William of Orange in the New Church in Delft **12** Part of the royal family **14** Statue of William II in The Hague **17** The golden coach **18** Some 350 companies have been granted a Royal Warrant, an honour for the quality of their products

language

Facts Dutch is spoken by about 22 million people in Europe • Outside Europe, about the same number speak Dutch or a daughter language • The Algemeen Woordenboek der Nederlandse Taal is the world's largest dictionary • Frisian is an official minority language

IT MAY HAPPEN IN INDONESIA THAT A PASSER-BY WILL INTRODUCE
HIMSELF IN DUTCH WITH THE WORDS, 'HELLO SIR, MY NAME IS HERMAN.
WOULD YOU MIND IF I SPOKE DUTCH WITH YOU FOR FIFTEEN MINUTES OR SO?'

The tongue twisters of the Low Countries

'Scheveningen', 'Schiermonnikoog': foreigners attempting to pronounce these place names are sure to torture their larynxes. And if they nonetheless wish to master the language, the helpful Dutch will thwart them by speaking to them only in their own language.

The hard *ch* sound is one of the biggest problems of Dutch for foreigners. With satanic delight, a Dutchman will serve up the most popular Dutch curse: *godverdomme* (goddamn). What's this? *Ch* and *g* have the same sound! How awful!

The same is true of *ei* and *ij*. The fact that *ij* occurs only in Dutch is an additional problem. Many Dutch companies and organisations have already adapted their names out of necessity, such as Rotterdam's football club Feyenoord (formerly Feijenoord).

An added complication for outsiders is that the hard *ch* sound and the *g* sound are soft in the south and east of the country. There are many dialects and regional languages in the Netherlands, often proudly upheld by their speakers. This is certainly the case among residents of the province of Friesland. Frisian, which is barely understood in the rest of the country, is recognised as an official minority language. Books are frequently published in Frisian and there is even a Frisian-Japanese dictionary.

Language is alive in the Netherlands. The Dutch like to read, and they read a lot: no other country has a greater density of bookshops. At 45 thousand pages, the *Algemeen Woordenboek der Nederlandse Taal* is the world's largest dictionary.

The Dutch language is constantly evolving as well. New expressions and foreign concepts are easily absorbed. Dutch words in turn have found their way into other languages as a result of trade and the country's colonial past. The most notorious example is the word *apartheid*, which is understood in much of the world. The same past forms the basis of the relatively extensive language skills of the Dutch. Aside from

> **At 45 thousand pages, the *Algemeen Woordenboek der Nederlandse Taal* is the world's largest dictionary.**

Dutch and English, they normally speak one or more other languages. This can be an obstacle to foreigners wishing to learn Dutch; if at all possible, the Dutch like to speak other people's languages to them.

Dutch is spoken in Europe by about 22 million people: about 16 million in the Netherlands, some 5 million in Belgium and another 80 thousand in the extreme north-western corner of France. It is also the official languages of the former colony of Surinam and of the Netherlands Antilles and Aruba, which are still part of the Kingdom of the Netherlands.

Afrikaans, spoken by about twenty million people in South Africa and Namibia, is an official daughter language of Dutch. It developed from the language of Dutch colonists and some indigenous languages, and can be understood with relative ease by Dutch speakers. In other areas with which the Netherlands has had intensive contact, the influence is limited to Dutch place names and street names and a few words and expressions, although it may happen in Indonesia that a passer-by will introduce himself in Dutch with the words, 'Hello sir, my name is Herman. Would you mind if I spoke Dutch with you for fifteen minutes or so?' ■

01 The famous 'Van Dale' dictionary
04 Old-fashioned primer 05 Frisian dictionary 06 Still not able to read Dutch? Foreign newspapers are for sale everywhere 07 Tongue-twisting place names

Virtually the entire Dutch landscape is man-made • Only four percent of the country consists of 'original' natural landscapes • Nevertheless, the Dutch countryside is surprisingly varied • In many areas, 'new' natural landscapes are being created • The tunnel of the high-speed rail link under the Green Heart area is the longest drilled tunnel in the world • The Dutch are DIY fanatics and world champion renovators

Myths The Dutch use milk to clean their pavements

01

orderliness

THE CUTTING OF DYKES AND DUNES TO RESTORE THE NATURAL FLOW OF WATERWAYS UNDERLINES THE STRONG CONVICTION OF THE DUTCH IN THE 'MALLEABILITY' OF THE NATURAL WORLD: IN AREAS BEREFT OF NATURAL BEAUTY, NATURE IS SIMPLY CREATED.

see also 📖 04 below sea level 📖 06 water 📖 10 polders 📖 40 the toilet 📖 70 gezelligheid

A carefully plotted-out country

No other country in the world is as much a product of planning and regulation as the Netherlands. The Dutch landscape has been designed right down to the last centimetre, as though it were a box of building blocks. The Dutch are just as neat and tidy when it comes to home improvements. And all interest groups are taken into account. Running out of nature? Then let's create some!

Taking a bird's eye view of the Netherlands, one particular character trait becomes immediately apparent. The viewer is treated to quilts of fields and meadows, separated only by straight waterways and beautifully arranged housing developments. It is order in its purest form. The Dutch leave nothing to chance when it comes to the design of their country. Passionate about the tape measure, they have created a neatly plotted-out paradise for themselves.

This passion for planning is rooted in the eternal struggle of the Dutch against water. Give the wet stuff free reign, and the Netherlands would soon be declared unfit for human habitation. The Netherlands also happens to be the most densely populated country of Europe. These factors have made organisation and regulation a bitter necessity.

The Dutch faced these challenges head-on. They have transformed the natural landscape and turned it into a neatly organised man-made landscape. The Netherlands is an architectural masterpiece, 'designed' down to the last detail. Only a minute portion of the country is in a natural state. But the country is not one big, monotonous meadow. The forests of the Veluwe, the Utrecht hills, the Drenthe moorland and the hills of Limburg are as Dutch as the polders, meadows and coastline.

So does the designer just sit back once he has finished his masterpiece? Certainly not! Throughout the 20th century, nature groups and environmental organisations were making their voices heard: the far-reaching regulations were gradually eroding the characteristic landscapes and impacting on plant and animal species, not to mention the quality of life. People started asking whether that was what we want.

Of course not. So nature reserves were created, new environmental protection laws enacted and forests replanted. In some areas, dykes and dunes were cut to allow waterways to retrace their natural course. Animal species that had disappeared, such as beavers and oxen, were reintroduced. 'Wildlife viaducts', 'ecoducts' and 'fauna passages' allowed wildlife to bypass traffic arteries in peace and safety. All these measures underline the strong conviction of the Dutch in the 'malleability' of the natural world: where there is no nature, nature can be created.

But quality of life and nature conservation involve balancing conflicting needs and interests. In such a densely populated country, conservation policies are often in conflict with the need for economic growth. Big infrastructural projects are virtually always compromises concluded after painstakingly slow consultations. The high-speed rail link through the so-called Green Heart of the Randstad conurbation and the freight line planned for 2007, linking Rotterdam to the German border, were only

> Home improvements have become a national hobby. Home improvement and garden centres are thriving.

01 Neighbours in Aagtekerke 02 Typical polder landscape near Lelystad 03 The Zuider Sea Museum in Enkhuizen

possible after incorporating hundreds of 'fauna passages' and tunnels in the plans, including the longest ever to have been drilled anywhere in the world.

The Dutch passion for order and regulation can also be seen in new urban districts and traffic plans. All traffic participants are catered for: each has its own set of traffic lights, and there are bicycle paths, zebra crossings, speed bumps and signposts aplenty. The much-needed new urban districts are not only a symbol of organisation, but sometimes also of suffocating uniformity. To improve the quality of life, architectural experiments are increasingly given free reign. This is of course always accompanied by extensive consultation exercises. Once again, compromises are sought, and the needs of all interested parties taken into account.

In their own homes and gardens, the Dutch are their own master architects. They are made for the part. The Netherlands is awash with drills and hammers, paint and wallpaper paste. And if there is nothing left to demolish or redecorate, then attentions soon shift to a new skylight, carport or pergola. Home improvements have become a national hobby, and home improvement and garden centres are thriving. Furniture retail parks are open on Easter Monday and Boxing Day, and are overrun by spendthrift families. Home improvement and gardening programmes are hugely popular.

This addiction to home improvements seems to be related to the changeable Dutch climate. When the weather is grim, the Dutch retreat to their cosy

homes. This domesticity is ably reflected in the Dutch saying '*Zoals het klokje thuis tikt, tikt het nergens*', or There's No Place Like Home. To the Dutch, the home is a safe haven, lovingly decorated with plants and knickknacks that help create that feeling of homeliness. Classic items such as the garden gnome and circular cut-out figures of swans which for years graced thousands of gardens and window boxes have long outstayed their welcome. The Dutch have turned their attention to having roofing tiles adorning the front door, depicting the family name in brightly coloured letters and the word 'Welcome'.

The home should be clean and tidy. This is a long-cherished ideal for the Dutch. An old travel guide to the Netherlands even proclaims that the Dutch clean their pavements with milk. To this day, many homes and gardens are a symbol of respectability; they are as neatly arranged as the countryside. And this neatness is there for all to see. To the amazement of many overseas visitors, the Dutch rarely draw their curtains at night, as if to say 'Feel free to look around and admire our plotted-out paradise.' ■

04-34 Interiors, decoration materials and bric-à-brac
21 Scouring powder 26 'No bicycles here!'

Facts The Dutch toilet bowl has caused many a tourist to flee the country in desperation • The Dutch view the toilet as the 'smallest room' in the house and like to make it cosy as a result

Myths The shape of the Dutch toilet bowl is related to a built-in tendency towards water management or a deep-rooted need to keep and order everything

01

TOILETS →

02   03   04

the toilet

ONE THING FOREIGNERS CAN AGREE ON: BEING ABLE TO SEE YOUR OWN WASTE, AND WANTING TO, IS A SIGN OF A TWISTED, ALMOST SICK NEED THAT IS CONTRARY TO ALL THAT IS CIVILISED. YUCK!

see also ▯ 36 orderliness ▯ 70 gezelligheid

Mysteries of the 'smallest room'

There is hardly a travel piece on the Netherlands that does not refer to the peculiarities of Dutch toilets and especially of the toilet bowl. Its vast plateau offers an unimpeded view of one's waste. Are the Dutch congenitally unclean or is the mystery connected to their built-in tendency towards water management?

'There's no doubt about it,' says an American. 'I've been living here long enough and I know the Dutch. If they can't see land above water, they're not happy'.

It's one of the many inspired theories put forward by foreigners to account for the unusual shape of the Dutch toilet bowl, which, unlike toilets in most other countries, are not dominated by a deep puddle of water, but by a plateau that is virtually dry. In technical terms, the Dutch toilet is a shallow flusher, not a deep flusher.

Tourists sometimes also associate the mystery with the deep-rooted urge of the Dutch to retain things and also their need to order and analyse everything. Commentators agree on one thing: they don't like it and often they are even shocked. Being able to, and wanting to, see one's own waste is a sign of some or other distasteful, twisted, almost sick need that is contrary to all that is civilised. Yuck!

And yet that is precisely one of the two reasons given by toilet experts for the popularity of the shallow flusher: a plateau is very useful for studying waste, which can come in handy, especially with children. The second reason is equally practical: the shallow flusher does not splash back on the user's buttocks. This has little to do with a built-in tendency to want to see 'land above water'.

Foreigners are astounded by Dutch toilet culture for an entirely different reason as well: the custom of toilet interior décor. The Dutch urge for domesticity and cosiness extends even to what is popularly known by the telling name of the 'smallest room'. The toilet is an integral part of the home and there is no reason not to make it *gezellig*, or cosy.

This is why toilets are at least neatly painted or wallpapered and decorated to some extent. The standard features include a mirror over the sink and a per-petual birthday calendar on the wall, usually flanked by a day-to-day calendar and a poster or some postcards or photos. There are often books, newspapers or magazines lying around, sometimes in a special cabinet; some toilets resemble outbuildings of a local library. The top of such a cabinet is a fine place for some plants and toilet paper bearing comic illustrations adds to the atmosphere. A final touch of *gezelligheid* is sometimes provided in the form of an old-fashioned Dutch tile on the wall with a humorous text. Now that's cosy! ■

Toilet experts say a plateau in the toilet bowl is very useful for studying waste.

01, 04 & 06 The famous Dutch shallow flusher **03** Lavatory attendant **05** Aliens using a modern street toilet **07** 'Occupied'

Facts The Netherlands is a paradise for those who love historic cities • It is also a trendsetter in modern architecture • Rotterdam is the Mecca of modern Dutch architecture • The Rietveld-Schröder house in Utrecht is on the UNESCO list of World Heritage Sites

Myths There is only interesting historic architecture in the Netherlands

architecture

SMALL-SCALE INNER CITIES WITH CANALS AND HISTORIC STRUCTURES, BUT ALSO SPECTACULAR MODERN BUILDINGS AND BRIDGES: THE DUTCH BUILDING TRADITION IS SURPRISINGLY RICH AND DIVERSE.

see also 16 canals 114 Rotterdam 118 Amsterdam

Trendsetting in every era

Foreigners associate the Netherlands primarily with charming historic inner cities and stately canalside houses. Yet it is as well an international trendsetter in modern architecture and urban construction. This means lovers of architecture have all kinds of options in the Netherlands.

Small-scale inner cities full of historic homes with masonry and striking façade crowns, lined by canals and greenery: tourists love it and the country's full of it. Amersfoort, Amsterdam, Buren, Delft, Deventer, Enkhuizen, Gouda, Groningen, Haarlem, The Hague, Hoorn, Kampen, Leiden, Maastricht, Middelburg, Naarden, Utrecht, Zutphen, Zwolle, Zierikzee – there are too many to mention.

In many of these places, the development of the inner city can still be easily traced. A canal would be dug around the historic core and there would be expansion around it, again ringed by a canal. Cities were also equipped with city walls and encircled by a canal called a *singel* to defend it. A small number of bridges and gates provided access to the city, which sometimes took on the appearance of a true fort in a characteristic star shape. The most beautiful example of this is the 16th-century Bourtange fort in the province of Groningen.

Light years removed from the redoubtable fort but speaking equally to the imagination is internationally renowned modern Dutch architecture. Its centre is Rotterdam, a city that was razed in 1940 by German bombers and that has since developed dynamically and daringly into a 'Manhattan on the Maas'. Daring architecture is also found in Almere, one of the new cities that arose in the 1960s on reclaimed land and which are planned right down to the paving tiles. But even outside these cities, the Netherlands is home to much talked-about 20th century architecture: housing and office estates, bridges, viaducts, waterworks, stadiums and railway stations have been the subject of much admiration abroad.

The countless striking structures in styles of which few or no examples are found outside the Netherlands are certainly remarkable. These include the brilliant designs from the first half of the 20th cen-

01 National Trade Unions Museum, Amsterdam **02** The miniature city of Madurodam in The Hague

Certainly remarkable are the countless striking structures in styles of which few or no examples can be found outside the Netherlands.

tury by Hendrik Berlage, one of the country's most famous architects, who inspired, and blazed a trail for, modern Dutch architecture.

Berlage's buildings are characterised by simplicity and functionality and are executed in brick. His most famous designs include the present day National Trade Unions Museum (1900) and the mercantile exchange (1903), both in Amsterdam, and the Sint-Hubertus hunting lodge in Hoge Veluwe national park. The last was commissioned by Mr and Mrs Kröller-Müller, merchants whose holdings in land and art formed the basis of the park and within it the Kröller-Müller museum with its famous Van Gogh collection.

The preference for brickwork was also a feature of the Amsterdam School. The imaginative towers, decorative doors and undulating rooflines of this style can be found in the Amsterdam Shipping House by Johan van der Mey and the brothers Van Gendt (1913) and Michel de Klerk's workers' homes in the Spaarndammer neighbourhood in Amsterdam (1916). Characteristics of this style, combined with art deco, can also be seen in the beautiful Tuschinski theatre in Amsterdam (1921), designed by Hijman de Jong.

A group of artists organized under the name *De Stijl* (The Style) produced revolutionary work. They espoused abstract form, based on straight lines and the use of a limited number of colours. The architects in the group used new material such as reinforced concrete and steel and sought to connect with the work of Frank Lloyd Wright and Le Corbusier, among others. The best-known structure in this style is the Rietveld-Schröder house in Utrecht, designed in 1924 by Gerrit Rietveld, which is on the UNESCO list of World Heritage Sites. Also famous is the De Unie café in Rotterdam by Jacobus Oud, of the same year.

Inspired by De Stijl but executed in yellow brick is the spectacular Hilversum town hall, designed by Willem Dudok (1931). Johannes Brinkman and Leendert van der Vlugt's design for the Van Nelle factory in Rotterdam in the *Nieuwe Bouwen* (New Building) style (1931) was also groundbreaking.

As a reaction to functionalist building, there was a return to natural forms and materials such as bricks and wood. A much-discussed example of this 'organic building' is the head office of Gasunie in Groningen, completed in 1994, designed by Ton Alberts and Max van Huut.

The 1990s reinforced the Netherlands' trendsetting reputation in modern architecture. There has been praise all round for one of the world's most famous architects, Rem Koolhaas, who built the Kunsthal exhibition centre (1992), among other structures, in his native Rotterdam. The city also saw the creation of the impressive Erasmus bridge in 1996, linking the south shore of the Maas with the city centre. Ben van

Berkel's design was at the same time a link to the 21st century, when Dutch architects will continue to attract international attention. ■

Facts The Netherlands has over 1100 mills • Only a fraction of those mills is still in daily use • The nineteen Kinderdijk windmills are a World Heritage Site • De Noord in Schiedam is the tallest mill in the world • The windmill helped transform the 17th century Zaanstreek into the first industrial region in the world • The legendary boxer Bep van Klaveren (1907 – 1992) was known as *The Dutch Windmill*

Myths The windmill is a Dutch invention

01

windmills

THE DUTCH NO LONGER DEPEND ON THE WIND FOR THEIR LIVELIHOOD. THE ONE THOUSAND ONE HUNDRED REMAINING WINDMILLS HAVE NEVERTHELESS HELPED UPHOLD THE REPUTATION OF THE NETHERLANDS AS THE WINDMILL CAPITAL OF THE WORLD.

see also 04 below sea level 06 water 10 polders

Land of wind and sails

For centuries, the Dutch depended on the wind for their livelihoods. While Dutch merchants were busy sailing the seas, the windmills back home were helping to drain the polders and to create and maintain a versatile industry. By the time the Steam Age hit the Netherlands, the country had over eleven thousand mills. Only 1100 remain, enough to uphold the country's image as the windmill capital of the world. Nowadays however, visitors to the Netherlands are more likely to see a modern wind turbine in action than a traditional one.

Ask any tourist to name a characteristic Dutch building, and chances are he will reply: the windmill. This is quite understandable. After all, a Dutch landscape without windmills is inconceivable. Interestingly however, the traditional Dutch windmill is not a Dutch invention. The first windmills to surface in this flat, wind-rich country in the 13th century are thought to be based on a Persian prototype, or 'blown over' via Spain from North Africa or the Middle East. Admittedly, the Netherlands already had fully operational mills before the year 1000, but these were watermills, used to grind corn. The first windmills were corn mills, too. In the first half of the 14th century, windmills were deployed to drain polders. The first polder mills were subjected to a host of modifications and improvements. The result? A mind-boggling array of windmill types. One particularly revolutionary Dutch invention was the so-called *bovenkruier* (cap winder),

the sails of which are attached to a small, rotating cap. Previously, the entire mill house had to be set facing the wind – backbreaking work.

The most impressive collection of polder mills can be found at Kinderdijk. This site is home to nineteen 18th century windmills, which were used until 1950 to prevent the drained Alblasserwaard from flooding. The Kinderdijk windmills have been included on the UNESCO World Heritage List and are one of the most photographed attractions in the country.

As well as polder windmills, the Netherlands also has industrial windmills, dating back to the late 16th century. The biggest concentration of windmills is in the Zaanstreek (Zaan area), the oldest industrial region in the world. It was here that the first saw mills surfaced in 1596, creating a rich and varied industry. The inventor, Cornelis Corneliszoon, initially tried to sell his prototype sawmill to the people of Amsterdam. He was met with heavy opposition from the guild of hand sawyers. In the Zaanstreek, sawmills were a tremendous boost to the shipbuilding industry. The shipyards of the Zaanstreek became world famous. In 1697, the Russian tsar Peter the Great even travelled incognito to Zaandam to study shipbuilding.

The number of industrial windmills in the Zaanstreek mushroomed. In the mid 17th century, there were six

01 The Zaanse Schans near Zaandam **04** Miller inside the windmill De Nieuwe Palmboom in Schiedam **05** Windmill in Westzaan

hundred. By the 18th century, the number was rumoured to be around one thousand. These windmills were used for sawing Norwegian and German wood, mixing pigments, grinding marble, scutching hemp, pressing oils, grinding tobacco and milling paper, lead and food and luxury foods such as cocoa, mustard and grain. The windmills were situated in the towns and towered above the houses, enabling them to make maximum use of the wind. The tallest surviving windmill is located not in the Zaanstreek, but in Schiedam: De Noord, measured from the tip of its top sail, measures over 44 metres in height, making it

the tallest windmill in the world.

The most beautiful collection of Zaanse industrial windmills can be found along the Zaanse Schans. The seven windmills and surrounding traditional artisan businesses and houses are largely from other parts of the Zaanstreek, and rebuilt along the Schans. Although they are open to the public, they are not museums; they are used to live in and work in, a particularly fine *Zaans* tradition.

Of the 1100 remaining mills in the Netherlands – including over one hundred watermills – only a

Windmills helped the Zaanstreek become the first industrial region in the world.

handful are still in daily use. Over one hundred windmills are kept in operation at set times by amateur millers. However, windmill enthusiasts are more likely to see an ultra-modern wind turbine in action than a traditional windmill.

These turbines are dotted across the land: some near farms, where they tower over every single building, others clustered in big wind parks. Although the pancake-flat country appears ideal for wind-powered energy, it has so far failed to live up to that promise. Protests from environmental organisations, municipalities and local residents have stopped the turbines from popping up all over the country.

Maybe that's why the wind energy lobby took to the North Sea. Some 25 kilometres from the coast of the seaside resort of Egmond aan Zee the first Dutch offshore wind park will be constructed. This trial project will consist of 36 gigantic turbines, which are expected to supply power to over 110 thousand households. If the government and wind farm operators have their way, there will be many more and bigger 'sea wind parks' in the future. ■

06 Windmill at the Zaanse Schans 07 Baarlo, inside a water mill 08 Schiedam, the highest windmills of the world 09 Windmill De Bonte Hen at the Zaanse Schans near Zaandam 11 Windenergy in the Wadden Sea near the island of Texel 14 Festively decorated windmill 16 The famous windmills at Kinderdijk, included on the UNESCO World Heritage List

SHORT PERIOD OF REST

LONG PERIOD OF REST

IN MOURNING

REJOICING

Windmills communicate

Windmills are not only milling tools, they are also excellent communication aids. By positioning or decorating the sails in a certain way, millers could communicate specific messages. The uses varied from region to region. In the Zaanstreek for instance, the position of the sails informed the community not only of a death: the number of wind boards removed from the sails also indicated whether the deceased was the miller himself, his wife, or his child. During festive occasions, such as marriages or births, the sails were decorated with flags, sprigs of evergreens, streamers or other decorations. To this day, it is possible to tell from the position of the sails whether the windmill will be out of action for a longer or shorter period of time.

Facts The Netherlands is the only country in Europe where barrel organs can still be seen on the streets • A Belgian and a German are chiefly responsible for the popularity of the barrel organ culture • Sentimental Dutch songs owe their popularity partly to the barrel organ • Some exceptional barrel organs are protected by law

Myths The barrel organ is a Dutch invention • The coin tin is really an ashtray

01

barrel organs

ENJOY A SHOPPING SPREE ACCOMPANIED BY SENTIMENTAL DUTCH SONGS WITH THE ORGAN GRINDER SHAKING HIS COIN TIN IN TIME TO THE MUSIC!

Music on wheels

Sentimental Dutch songs like *Tulips from Amsterdam* owe their popularity partly to a special musical instrument: the barrel organ. The Netherlands is the only country in Europe where this distinctive instrument has not disappeared from the streets. However, it is not a Dutch invention. The main impetus for the barrel organ culture came from a Belgian and a German.

For many tourists it is rather like a close encounter of the third kind. As you stroll leisurely along the Amsterdam canalside streets admiring the handsome buildings, you suddenly find yourself face to face with an oddly shaped, extravagantly decorated musical instrument on wheels. It is impossible to ignore the piercing sounds emitted by this enormous beast, neither is it possible to ignore the owner as he rattles his coin tin rhythmically under your nose. Time to pay up!

Barrel organs are as Dutch as tulips and clogs. They are seldom seen on streets outside the Netherlands. Even so, the roots of this instrument do not lie in the Netherlands. The first street barrel organ probably emerged in Italy, where it was used to introduce opera to the common man. The little portable organs, which hung from a strap around the neck of the organ grinder or rested on a folding stand, soon became popular. Their size increased with their popularity, and by the end of the 19th century the organ on wheels could be heard all over Europe.

A Belgian called Leon Warnies was responsible for bringing the barrel organ to the Netherlands. He opened the first organ hire company in Amsterdam in 1875, and other hire companies soon followed. The organs were initially made in France, Germany and Belgium, but after 1920 the organ industry began to flourish in the Netherlands, when the German organ maker Carl Frei set up a business in Breda. Frei gave the instrument a new sound and continued to produce new compositions, giving the Dutch barrel organ culture a huge impulse.

Nowadays the Netherlands is the only country in Europe where barrel organs can still be seen on the streets. In city centres the Dutch do their shopping

01, 04 & 05 Barrel organ, owned by Mr Broers, Leiden **02** Organ books are a vital part of the barrel organ. The holes in these books define the pitch and the length of the tones **03** Detail from a barrel organ in the Van Speelklok tot Pierement Museum, Utrecht **06** The barrel organ *Hindenburg*, owned by G. Perlee, Amsterdam

One minute you are enjoying the Amsterdam canals and canalside houses, the next minute you are standing face to face with a strange musical instrument on wheels.

to the sounds of catchy traditional songs and original compositions by the organ grinder – and of course to the rhythm of the inescapable coin tin. With the exception of a few fervent organ haters, most people can appreciate the ambience. Barrel organs contribute to the typical Dutch concept of *gezellig*, a word widely used in Dutch to describe a pleasant atmosphere, whether convivial, cheerful, cosy, lively or friendly.

However, life can be difficult for organ grinders, and over the years many barrel organs have been sold to foreign collectors. In order to prevent the export of the more valuable organs, the government has labelled some instruments irreplaceable items of cultural significance. This averts the danger of the tradition being lost for ever, especially if local people and tourists continue to fill the coin tins! We certainly do not have to worry about the disappearance of the coin tin, as tens of thousands of these tins still exist. For many years they were popular as ashtrays in the *gezellig* Dutch living rooms. ∎

👍 **Facts** Clogs were once worn by the vast majority of Dutch people • The oldest Dutch clog dates from the 13th century • Nowadays, the Netherlands is more or less unclogged • Even so, a million clogs are sold annually • The clog business relies on tourism • During winter, the clogs are filled with straw and newspaper to keep the feet warm

📋 **Myths** The clog is a Dutch invention • All Dutch people wear clogs

clogs

ALTHOUGH THE NETHERLANDS ARE NOW UNCLOGGED, CLOGS DECORATED WITH HUMOROUS SAYINGS, A DOPE-SMOKING PEASANT GIRL OR THE NIKE LOGO ARE ON SALE EVERYWHERE.

see also 📄 **114** Rotterdam

Ancient symbol of an unclogged nation

You couldn't imagine the Netherlands without them, although only a limited number of Dutch people wear them: clogs. Despite this, clog manufacturers have their hands full. The wooden shoe, which probably originates from France, is an extremely popular souvenir with tourists.

Lots of people are under the misconception that all Dutch people wear clogs. Ask any passer-by, for instance in Sioux Falls, South Dakota, and they will say the same thing. Of course, this tells us something about the person questioned (who will just as easily claim that Holland is the capital of Scandinavia), but still: the international perception is of the Netherlands' indestructible bond with wooden footwear.
There was indeed a time when all Dutch people wore clogs, apart from the upper classes. They were particularly practical in the countryside, because of the boggy soil. During winter, they were filled with straw, as they still are in rural areas, with the addition of shredded newspaper.
The oldest clog around today dates from the 13th century. It was found in the dam that was built on the Rotte river at that time. Around that dam the city of Rotterdam, the second city of the Netherlands in terms of size, came into being. The clog is made of alder wood and can be admired in the city's historical museum.

There were skating clogs, football clogs, bridal clogs and even smuggler's clogs.

As far as we know, the clog is not a Dutch invention but a French one. However, the clog-making trade reached maturity in the Low Countries. Key factors in this were the enormous demand for them, and the fact that the ideal wood for clogs – willow and poplar – were available in abundance.
Though the modern-day, standard yellow clog would lead you to believe otherwise, the clog makers developed their own models, motifs and decorations. Furthermore, there was demand for special clogs for all kinds of purposes. There were ice clogs (with spikes underneath), skating clogs, clogs for playing football in, bridal clogs and even smuggler's clogs. The latter left prints which did not betray the direction of the wearer, but pointed in another direction.
Clogs are not worn very often today. This is due to the sharp reduction in the number of Dutch people working in agriculture and cattle-farming. The handful of cheese porters and folkloric companies who had just discovered them was too small to counter the unclogging of the Netherlands.
Even so, clog makers still do a good trade. Their customers are no longer peasants looking for the newest skating clog, or inhabitants of the borderlands looking for new smuggling clogs, but more likely Japanese, Americans and Germans searching for a typical Dutch souvenir. A million are sold each year, and the variety of what is on offer is staggering. Clogs are available in the colours of the Dutch national flag,

01 Going Dutch: tourists from Singapore disguished as fishermen in a photo studio in Volendam

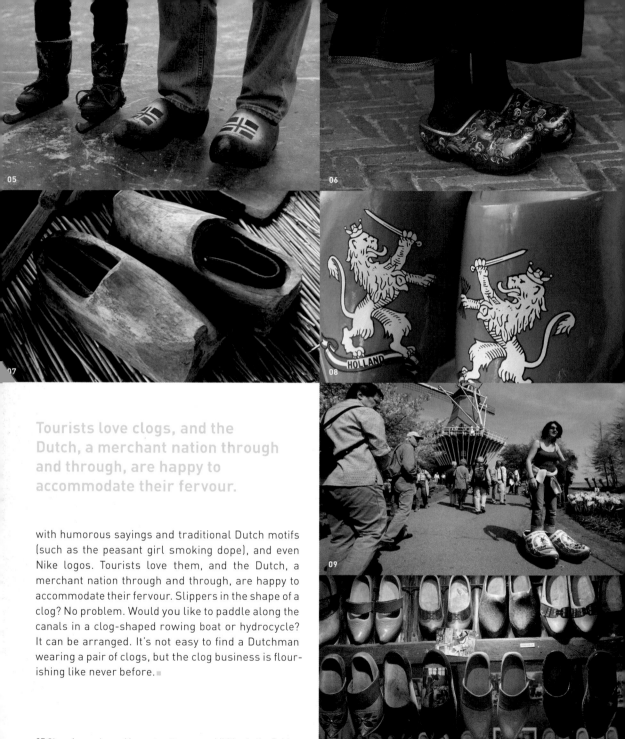

Tourists love clogs, and the Dutch, a merchant nation through and through, are happy to accommodate their fervour.

with humorous sayings and traditional Dutch motifs (such as the peasant girl smoking dope), and even Nike logos. Tourists love them, and the Dutch, a merchant nation through and through, are happy to accommodate their fervour. Slippers in the shape of a clog? No problem. Would you like to paddle along the canals in a clog-shaped rowing boat or hydrocycle? It can be arranged. It's not easy to find a Dutchman wearing a pair of clogs, but the clog business is flourishing like never before. ■

07 Clogs formerly used by peat cutters, on exhibition in the Polder Museum in Noorden **09** Kingsize clogs at the Keukenhof, the world's largest flower garden **11** Going Dutch Part II

Facts The Netherlands has four million cows and thirty thousand dairy farms • The Dutch dairy cow produces 35 litres every day: a world record • Dairy farming is a hypermodern industry • The semen of the best breeding bulls sells for huge sums of money • The average Dutch person eats 22 kilograms of beef a year

Myths The cow is a sacred animal in the Netherlands • The term 'bio-industry' guarantees animal-friendly treatment

01

02	03	04	05

COWS

WITH AN AVERAGE PRODUCTION OF 35 LITRES A DAY, THE MOTHER OF ALL DAIRY COWS GRAZES IN A DUTCH FIELD.

see also 78 Dutch cuisine 82 cheese

The land of *Mooo!*

Celebrated as the world champion of milk production and cherished as the national favourite animal the Dutch cow is almost sacred. The statues erected here and there speak volumes: the Dutch are proud of this die-hard symbol of Dutch prosperity. This love affair does not run deep, however. The Dutch like their steaks.

Green pastures of happily grazing cattle, under a beautiful cloudy sky: you won't find a more Dutch landscape. It's an image the tourists appreciate, as do the Dutch. And one that can be found everywhere in the green quilted landscape of four million cows and thirty thousand dairy firms that is the Netherlands. The fact that the cow is a national symbol is indelibly stamped on the collective Dutch psyche. Cows are cherished more than the tulip or the clog. This privileged treatment is probably due to their visibility and the fact that no other symbol is as cuddly as a cow. With her disarming expression, the Dutch have embraced her as the national favourite animal.

Furthermore, the friendly giant brings in a lot of money. The dairy trade – another national symbol – is a good earner. Forty per cent of the national herd are dairy cows, which is considerably more than in neighbouring countries. And with an average milk production of 35 litres, the Dutch seem to possess the mother of all dairy cows; an absolute world champion.

The dairy industry is a very serious and highly advanced one, though you wouldn't say so watching the traditional ritual of haggling between farmer and market trader. Hypermodern breeding methods are deployed to continuously improve the quality of the cattle. Like the dairy products themselves, the semen of breeding bulls is an important export product. The best bulls' semen sells for incredible amounts of money.

Nothing is left to chance as far as the Dutch cow's glowing reputation is concerned. Part of this fame has been earned by the world-famous Frisian pedigree cattle, which long afforded the Frisian farmer an unassailable position in the world of cattle and dairy exports. How they laughed in the other provinces, and indeed other parts of the world, when they were able to breed cattle that equalled or even bettered the quality of the pedigree cow. Nevertheless, the Frisians felt their loyal milk producer deserved a statue. It can be seen in the Frisian capital, Leeuwarden, and bears the telling inscription 'Our Mother'. The Frisians are not alone in their worship, as statues of cows have been erected elsewhere in the country.

However, the Dutch are no strangers to a certain kind of hypocrisy. For despite all the statues, there is also a large-scale bio-industry, to which the term 'animal-

> ## The statue of the Frisian pedigree cow bears the telling inscription, 'Our Mother'.

friendly' could not be applied. Every year, a million cows and 1.5 million calves are slaughtered, most of them totally unaware of the existence of grassy pastures. A Dutch person consumes 22 kilograms of beef every year without batting an eyelid. There's nothing sacred about this national favourite animal; the Dutch sacred cow does not have four legs but four wheels. Luckily though, more and more Dutch people are of a different opinion. ∎

02 Dutch milk from dairy cooperative Campina **07** 'Small cow's' chocolate bar

01

cycling

EVEN THE DUTCH GOVERNMENT ALWAYS INCLUDES A COUPLE OF MINISTERS WHO TRAVEL TO WORK BY BIKE, TO EMPHASISE JUST HOW NORMAL THEY REALLY ARE – A VERY DUTCH TRAIT.

see also 16 canals

Born on two wheels

The Netherlands is the bicycle capital of the world. It has more bicycles than inhabitants and has the highest bicycle density in the world. The steel steed is also a solution for visitors whose motto is 'going native': rent a bike and go! But watch out for tram rails, and make sure you have a solid lock, as the Netherlands also has the world's highest density of bicycle thieves.

Are the Dutch born on two wheels? Some people seem to think so. With its twenty million bikes to 16 million inhabitants, the Netherlands can boast the highest density of bicycles in the world, which makes an impression everywhere. In a Hindu temple in Bali, in the former Dutch colony of Indonesia, one can even see a relief of a cycling Dutchman.

Many Dutch people own several bikes: a 'decent' one for going on trips, and a 'regular' one – usually an old wreck – for daily use, like shopping. In large cities in particular, few Dutch people are prepared to park their smart bikes just anywhere, as there is a strong chance that they will have to walk home; the Netherlands also has the world's highest density of bicycle thieves. Some 800 thousand bikes are stolen every year, which is quite a record.

This is why the Dutch prefer to use several locks to secure their bicycles to trees, fences, bridges and lampposts. Not that this bothers the professional tooled up with a pair of concrete shears and an angle grinder, but the vast majority of bicycle thieves are drug addicts for whom 'scoring' a couple of bikes is a quick method of getting hold of drugs. The stolen goods are sold on at bargain prices, and the fact that the trade in secondhand bikes is flourishing does not necessarily mean much money is being made.

The question of why the Netherlands is so devoted to the bicycle has never been answered satisfactorily. The fact is that the vehicle is not a Dutch invention, but a French or British one. The Dutch mania for cycling has much to do with the flatness of the country, although there are other flat regions where people don't cycle as much. Dutch children are hoisted onto a tricycle at an early age. Not long after, they receive their first 'grown up' bike and take their first

04 'Bicycles will be removed'

proficiency tests at infant school. The test results in an actual certificate, which along with swimming certificates adorns many a child's bedroom wall.

Things get serious when the children go to secondary school. Youngsters who cycle twenty kilometres through wind and hail are not unusual. Later on, the appeal of a moped, scooter or car is hard to resist, but even so many Dutch people stay loyal to their bikes. Some companies encourage their employees to cycle, and a flat tyre is the 'Dutchest' excuse there is for arriving late for work. Even the Dutch government always includes a couple of ministers who travel to work by bike, to emphasise just how normal they

Many cyclists are not content with the cycle paths; they want the entire road.

really are. It's a very Dutch trait, although in the eyes of some, administrators who parade their normality are abnormal.

The big Dutch bike manufacturers Gazelle, Batavus, Union and Sparta sell more than a million bicycles a year and do all they can to keep the bike in style. The solid workhorse that is known as the 'upright bicycle' has made way for a range of up-to-date models for the fashion and identity-conscious cyclist, from city bikes and all terrain bikes to reclining bicycles and bikes with auxiliary engines. Kids can strike a pose in tough cycling helmets, while parents do the same with the latest gadgets in the world of toddler transportation.

And the Netherlands wouldn't be the Netherlands without far-reaching consideration of the cyclists and their national pressure group. There are special traffic lights for cyclists, and cycle paths almost everywhere, covering over twenty thousand kilometres in total. Every shopping centre and railway station has its own bicycle rack and the number of tourist cycling routes runs into hundreds.

You'd think the cyclist would feel privileged with all these facilities at his disposal, but this is far from the case. Many of them are not content with the cycle paths; they want the entire road: they slalom through the traffic, ride without putting their hands on the handlebars, or without lights at night, and refuse to put out their hands to indicate when turning. This is the reason for the silent war between cyclists and motorists, which causes a mild identity crisis in many Dutch people, who are by turns both motorists and cyclists.

Because of this anarchic behaviour, most foreign visitors restrict themselves to a safe hydrocycle trip around the canals. Nonetheless, a trip by rented bike is the only real way to become a 'Dutchman among the Dutch'. Do make sure you don't get your wheels stuck in the tram rails, as the outcome of such incidents is rarely good.

Pedestrians, too, have no end of trouble with the Dutch bike culture. Foreigners regularly meet accidents when crossing the road, unused as they are to the silent vehicle. And a stroll through somewhere like Amsterdam quickly becomes more of an obstacle course through the fallen and badly-parked bicycles. However, the pinnacle of astonishment is the dredging of the romantic canals of Amsterdam: invariably, dozens of dumped bicycles are brought to the surface. 'Old love doesn't rust', goes a Dutch saying. This does not apply to the bicycle. ■

08 In the Hoge Veluwe national park visitors may use white 'park bikes' for free **09** Logo of Dutch bike manufacturer Gazelle **12** Formula-1 bike **13** Posing on a giant signpost

Facts Delft became world-famous thanks to Delft blue ceramics • The famous earthenware is modelled on Chinese porcelain • Delft blue is still crafted in the same manner • But beware of imitations: it is widely copied

Myths Delft blue ceramics are an original Delft creation • All Delft blue ceramics come from Delft

DELFT

05

Delft blue ceramics

DELFT POTTERS CONQUERED THE WORLD WITH THEIR IMITATIONS OF CHINESE PORCELAIN. DELFT BLUE CERAMICS ARE NOW IN TURN BEING BUSILY COPIED.

A genuine Dutch imitation

A windmill, a plate, a bowl or a tile. White with a subtle decoration in blue, preferably a Dutch landscape. Delft blue ceramics are sought-after souvenirs. The city of Delft became world-famous for its artistic earthenware, but it is not an original Delft creation: local potters copied the Chinese.

From its founding in 1602, the famous Dutch East India Company controlled trade with east Asia for more than 150 years. Following the example of the Portuguese, the world's first multinational imported items from China and it was thus that the Netherlands encountered Chinese porcelain in the early 17th century.

This encounter was not an entirely happy one. Because of the influx of increasingly popular porcelain, Dutch potters were barely able to sell their traditional products. The ceramics industry experienced great difficulty and many producers saw no option but to shut up shop.

A small number of manufacturers took on the Chinese competition and attempted to imitate their fragile porcelain. This was tricky, as the raw material and the process were unknown, but the Dutch came quite close: they succeeded in creating earthenware that was lighter, resembled porcelain and also had the characteristic white colour through the use of a new glaze. In addition to the usual Dutch depictions, eastern motifs were imitated in the blue of Chinese porcelain. In the mid-1600s, the Chinese inadvertently gave their Dutch competitors a helping hand, as the demise of the Ming dynasty caused Asian imports to decline. Delft manufacturers saw their chance: production was intensified, new factories opened and Delft blue ceramics conquered Europe. Seventeenth-century tile tableaux, vases and all manner of practical objects with the characteristic blue decoration can even be found in the palaces of Indian maharajahs, all of it made in Delft. Incidentally, the potters also used other colours, especially in the late 17th century.

Delft blue ceramics are still made in the traditional manner and guided tours of De Porceleyne Fles, a company founded in Delft in 1653, are popular. Other manufacturers in Delft, and in Gouda as well, also provide a view of the history and manufacturing of this famous, fragile earthenware. And of course, no souvenir shop is without Delft blue ceramics. But beware: the ceramics are imitated by unscrupulous manufacturers, so check the bottom to see that it doesn't happen to say *Made in China*. ∎

Seventeenth-century tile tableaux and practical objects with the characteristic blue decoration can even be found in the palaces of Indian maharajahs, all of it made in Delft.

01 Modern Delft blue, designed by Dutch Publishers **02, 03, 05 & 07** Painter and products at De Koninklijke Porceleyne Fles in Delft, a well-known manufacturer of Delft blue ceramics **04** Mural by Hugo Kaagman in Delft blue style on the wall of the Central Museum in Utrecht, called *Bush Miller/Murderer*. It criticizes an American bombing raid, by order of President Bush Sr., on the Libyan capital Tripoli in the early nineties

Dutch design

MARLIES DEKKERS, THE 'DIVA OF THE G-STRING', GAVE LINGERIE A NEW, HIGHLY SEDUCTIVE LOOK WITH HER DESIGNS.

👍 **Facts** Dutch design is celebrated for its functionality and simplicity • New York's airports use Dutch signposts • Major fashion brands such as Diesel, Nike and Tommy Hilfiger employ many Dutch designers • Dutch paper money was a paragon of handsome graphic design

👎 **Myths** Lowland sobriety and design are mutually exclusive • The Dutch don't care about clothes and know nothing about fashion

see also 📖 106 Made in Holland

Sober, practical and world-famous

Practical, simple and recognisable: these are the characteristics of Dutch design that make it big abroad. At home, there is less appreciation. The Dutch are just used to practical, sober solutions. Preferably with a dash of humour and elegance, but useable above all.

Dutch design is held in high regard abroad. Whether it's Philips shavers, the design and layout of Daf trucks or graphic design and typography, Dutch designs are famous for their functionality and simplicity. Even the Dutch tax return – not a product that is quick to elicit applause – is feted for its clear layout.

Dutch designers are generally averse to superfluous frills. An elegant design will be chosen if possible, and a little humour would be nice, but the most important aspects are practicality and ease of use. This formula means that Dutch design is highly recognisable.

The Dutch themselves view these sober designs soberly. The roadside assistance phone, the dual post-box and the litter bin, they are praised only in limited circles. They are functional solutions to everyday problems, and isn't that the whole point? 'Acting normally is crazy enough', is a Dutch proverb that is as old as it is profound.

One area where Dutch designers have been pointing the way internationally is signposts. The best example is the signage at Schiphol, the world's first major airport to have clear signposts. The chosen system of colour codes and large signs, developed by Bureau Mijksenaar, has now also been introduced

to New York's three major airports. An even bigger compliment to its designers was film director Steven Spielberg's invitation to provide 'Schiphol' signs for a recreation of an airport for his film *The Terminal*. More recent is the rise in Dutch fashion design. The

> ## The Dutch tax return – not a product that is quick to elicit applause – is feted for its clear layout.

practical, casual style of the Dutch does not elicit high praise from most foreigners, but Dutch fashion designers are in demand worldwide for their creativity and ability to design clothing that is both attractive and practical. Major brands such as Diesel, Nike and Tommy Hilfiger employ many Dutch designers; Dutch brands such as Gsus, Mexx, SO, Oilily and No-No are internationally successful, as are the collections of designers like Viktor & Rolf, Aziz and Marlies Dekkers, the 'Diva of the G-string', whose designs gave lingerie a new and highly seductive look. ∎

01 Couch 'Bird' 02 Information system at Schiphol airport 03 Chair 'Hanna' 04 Old DAF cars at the DAF Museum in Eindhoven 05 Urinal 'Kisses' 06 Phone booth 'Sidonia' 07 'Twinbox' letterbox 08 Lingerie by Marlies Dekkers 09 Philishave 10 'The Sunflower', banknote of fifty guilders, designed by R.D.E. Oxenaar for De Nederlandsche Bank **Detailed information and credits, see back flap**

Lost icons

Many Dutch people look back wistfully on their 'own' banknotes, replaced by the euro in 2002. Dutch paper money was a paragon of imagination and taste and brought the quality of Dutch graphic design to the attention of the world. The guilder notes of designers such as R.D.E. Oxenaar and Jaap Drupsteen that came into circulation starting in the 1960s were distinguished by their ease of recognition and daring use of colour. The way that figures from Dutch history were depicted was a shocking break with European monetary tradition: not stately or elitist, but stylised. Later, the national figures and symbols disappeared completely from banknotes. In their place came colourful ornaments, lighthouses and sunflowers. No wonder that most Dutch people still long for the cherished guilder and view the dull euros as a daily insult.

01

Dutch masters

FOR MANY YEARS REMBRANDT WAS IN GREAT DEMAND, BUT HIS ORIGINAL, AT TIMES DARING COMPOSITIONS OFTEN BROUGHT HIM INTO CONFLICT WITH HIS RICH CLIENTS, SOME OF WHOM REFUSED TO PAY HIM.

Brilliant but penniless

Their works sell for astronomical sums of money, but they themselves died poor and underrated. Many of the famous Dutch masters only received the recognition they deserved long after their death. Some, including Rembrandt, made a decent living. However, their artistic genius did not make them financial wizards.

The 17th century is generally regarded as the high point in the history of Dutch painting. During this 'Golden Age', the Netherlands dominated international trade. It was the richest country of Northwestern Europe, and Amsterdam became the commercial capital of the world.

The resulting prosperity and wealth was a major driving force behind the blossoming cultural life of the Netherlands. Painting in particular flourished, as is ably demonstrated by the collections of the main Dutch museums. The rich burghers commissioned painting after painting from such illustrious names as Frans Hals, Jan Steen, Jacob van Ruysdael and Pieter de Hoogh.

The most famous of all was the miller's son Rembrandt van Rijn (1606-1669), who in 1630 left his home town of Leiden to live and work in Amsterdam. From 1639 on he lived in the house which is known today as the Rembrandthuis Museum. He produced a wealth of paintings, etchings and drawings.

For many years, Rembrandt was in great demand. However, his original, at times daring compositions frequently brought him into conflict with his well-heeled clients, some of whom refused to pay him. Gradually, he fell out of grace with the powerful regents of Amsterdam.

A similar fate befell Rembrandt's most famous painting, *The Nightwatch*. Contrary to popular belief, the painting does not portray a night-time scene, but a division of the civic guard during the day. The original title of the painting was *The Civic Guard Company of Captain Frans Banning Cocq and Lieutenant Willem van Ruytenburch*. It was not until much later, when the varnish had darkened, that the painting was renamed. Civic guard members were generally well-heeled men. In the 17th century, their officers were clambering to have their portrait painted, turning civic guard paintings into a famous genre.

Rembrandt is reputed to have produced the enormous painting under a lean-to in his garden. No sooner had he completed his masterpiece (1642), than the problems began. Rather than portray the men seated nicely in a row or enjoying a festive meal, as was customary at the time, he had portrayed them in action. Each Civic Guard member was expected to pay Rembrandt one hundred guilders. However, some were so disappointed and outraged that they simply refused to pay.

A string of other misadventures amply demonstrates how people at the time viewed one of the most famous paintings in the world. Initially, it was put on display in the headquarters of the civic guard. In 1715, the painting was donated to the town hall, but was too big to fit between two windows. Ruthlessly unscrupulous, the new owners carved their knives through the painting. Strips of up to sixty centimetres were cut from all sides. Three of the 33 portrayed members of the civic guard perished during the operation.

Despite ongoing problems with his clients, Rembrandt was able to make a decent living. However,

01 A family in Nuenen during dinner. The tableau resembles the famous painting *The Potato Eaters*, which Vincent van Gogh painted in the same village **02** Prince Maurits, son of William of Orange; detail of a painting at the Prinsenhof Museum in Delft

this particular Dutch master was not a financial wizard. His passion for art was the source of many financial problems. He was a fervid collector of international art treasures and countless works of art of prominent painters. His bankruptcy forced him to sell his art collection and his house. Rembrandt died penniless, and was buried in a nameless grave in the Amsterdam Westerkerk.

Johannes Vermeer (1632-1675), Rembrandt's Delft-based contemporary, did not fare much better. His works were displayed on a bakery wall as collateral to cover his debts. Vermeer died penniless, a complete unknown. Only thirty-five of his paintings have survived. He left a wife, eleven children and a mountain of debt. Only long after his death did his work receive the recognition it deserved.

The end of the Golden Age did not mark the end of Dutch painting. The

In the early 20th century, paintings by Vincent van Gogh sold for pennies at a Dutch market.

most famous modern painter of the Low Countries is undoubtedly Vincent van Gogh (1853-1890), whose personal, powerful work continues to fire the imagination of millions.

Van Gogh's career as an artist spanned a mere ten years, during which he produced an impressive collection of paintings. In the last two years of his life alone, while living in the Provençal town of Arles, he produced over four hundred works of art. His fiercely coloured, emotionally charged later paintings contrast sharply with his darker, melancholic early work.

The life of Van Gogh is a classic tale of the tragic artist. Living in abject poverty, he was regularly malnourished. He was a highly sensitive, probing, lonely and at times desperate man. While in France, he was admitted twice to a mental asylum, suffering from severe psychological problems. In 1888, following an argument with his friend Paul Gauguin, he used a razor blade to cut off his left ear lobe.

Van Gogh committed suicide in 1890, having sold just one painting. Thirteen years later, his paintings were selling for as little as five cents apiece in the market of Breda. It was to take another forty years for his work to be recognised. Nowadays, Vincent van Gogh is universally considered to be one of the founding fathers of 20th century painting. Astronomical amounts are now paid for his paintings.∎

03 *The Nightwatch*, Rembrandt's most famous painting, at the Rijksmuseum [National Museum] in Amsterdam 04 A modern 'Vermeer girl' at the town hall in Delft, the city where Vermeer lived 05 *The Room of Escher* in the Escher Museum in The Hague. Maurits Escher (1898-1972) was a master of optical illusion 07 The grave of Johannes Vermeer in the Old Church in Delft 08 The Catharina Gasthuis Museum in Gouda 09 Galerij Prins Willem V in The Hague, the oldest public museum in the Netherlands, formerly the private collection of Prince William V 10 Vincent van Gogh look-alike 11 Van Gogh seems nearby in the house of farmer Theodorus Swinkels in Nuenen, where time stood still. Van Gogh lived and worked in Nuenen 12 Restoring a Vermeer painting

01

'gezelligheid'

AN INVITATION TO HAVE A *BAKKIE* CAN MEAN ONLY ONE THING: WE'RE GOING TO HAVE A NICE CHAT! THE FACT THAT THERE WILL ALSO BE COFFEE HAS MERELY RITUAL SIGNIFICANCE.

see also 36 orderliness 40 the toilet 74 Sinterklaas

The Dutch sense of well-being

It is a typically Dutch concept, one that is difficult to translate: *gezelligheid*. It is a term often used in the Netherlands, as life must be made as *gezellig* as possible. *Gezelligheid* is found in a setting that has atmosphere and in fun activities, but above all in the right company. Having a *bakkie* together is by definition *gezellig*.

The Dutch are companionable sorts. If at all possible, life should be convivial and cosy, but what makes it *gezellig*?

Having a *bakkie* – a cup of coffee, that is – is something one does with another person, possibly two others, but certainly not alone. Most Dutch people see drinking coffee alone as something that is not *gezellig* and it does not become such until a neighbour drops by. This can mean only one thing: we're going to have a nice chat! The fact that there will also be coffee has merely ritual significance.

So *gezelligheid* has to do with togetherness and companionship, but not every gathering is *gezellig*. A birthday party where no one talks is not *gezellig*. The conversation in which your boss gives you the sack is not at all *gezellig*.

Another foundation underlying the concept of *gezelligheid* is the Dutch sense of domesticity. The Dutch do everything to make their homes *gezellig* so that residents feel secure and at ease. Some like to surround themselves with collections of kitschy porcelain, others like to keep things as bare as possible. Plants, flowers and a fireplace or stove are things that make most Dutch people feel at home. If the occupants of the home gather to play a game or watch television, or if friends come to visit, *gezelligheid* is guaranteed and it easily becomes a late night. *Gezelligheid*, according to a popular saying, knows no time.

Pets also contribute to *gezelligheid*, they bring diversion and atmosphere, according to many people in the Netherlands. As long as they're not the neighbours'

01 Bulb growers selling flowers from their caravan near Lisse
07 When the weather allows, the pavement cafés are packed until late in the evening

ROODKAPJE

DE koffie is klaar

cats, that is – the ones who do their business in your garden with a devilish sense of satisfaction. Dogs relieving themselves on your front doorstep are not *gezellig* either. To combat this inconvenience, some municipalities introduced special 'dog toilets', areas where dogs could run free, but to no avail. In a last-ditch effort to maintain order, some town centres have been declared off-limits to man's best friend.

Millions of cats and dogs have the run of Dutch living rooms, along with a herd of rabbits, guinea pigs and feathered friends. The extent to which pets are taken seriously is illustrated by the dog-walking service found in almost every area. For injured pets, there is the animal ambulance.

Other animals also contribute to *gezelligheid*. Taking the kids to the pond to feed the ducks is *gezellig* by definition, as is a visit to a children's farm, where toddlers acquire their first exposure to nature amid a handful of deer, a wandering pig, a dozen rabbits and some ducks.

Things can also be *gezellig*, then, outside the home. The *café* is a traditional source of *gezelligheid*, particularly for regulars: surrounded by friends and acquaintances, there is always conversation and often card games or billiards. 'Brown cafés' get their name from the wooden décor and furniture, long associated with homeliness and conviviality. But time is taking its toll and many in the Netherlands now prefer the modern *grand café*, with its aura of design, its potted palms and fashionable food.

> **The Dutch take every opportunity to create gezelligheid.**

Most other activities outside the home are not *gezellig* until they are done with others: having something to eat, lounging on a patio or going to a film are typical social activities for most Dutch people. Characteristic is also that activities in clubs and associations are more popular in the Netherlands than anywhere else. The Dutch like to share their interests and have a well-developed sense of belonging.

The same type of camaraderie as is found in clubs still thrives in some neighbourhoods. Although neighbourhoods have lost much of their binding function in the western world, street parties are organised in some places. The national 'children's play day' is also used in many places to reinforce a sense of belonging, just as the Dutch take every opportunity to create *gezelligheid*. A fiftieth birthday is generally seen as an excellent excuse for a celebration and anniversaries customarily turn out to be major parties with food, sketch comedy and a master of ceremonies.

The ultimate in *gezelligheid* are the stag and hen parties, when the bride- and bridegroom-to-be celebrate their last 'unattached' evening, separately. Friends take the couple on an endless pub crawl and do everything to get them to the registry office in a state of inebriation, preferably dressed as a gorilla and a lady of the night. This is a form of *gezelligheid* that is not appreciated by everyone. That's why it is increasingly common for the couple to be allowed a period between the stag and hen parties and the wedding, so that they can sleep off their hangovers in a *gezellig* manner.∎

10 Scene at the Efteling in Kaatsheuvel, a very popular and renowned fairy tale attraction park **14** The game of goose, incredibly popular in the past and still a symbol of *gezelligheid* **15** The *bakkie* [cup of coffee] is the perfect excuse for *gezelligheid* **17** 'Coffee is being served'

Facts Sinterklaas is the most popular family holiday • Sinterklaas really exists (according to children) • Sinterklaas does not exist (according to adults) • The average Dutch household spends 130 euro on Sinterklaas presents • The Dutch also devour 9.4 million kilos of Sinterklaas sweets • Sinterklaas was the model for Father Christmas

Myths Sinterklaas lives in Spain • Sinterklaas stuffs naughty children into a burlap sack and takes them to Spain

01

Sinterklaas

IN ONE OF THE MOST BEAUTIFUL DUTCH TRADITIONS, THE MAIN ROLES ARE PLAYED BY A BISHOP ON HORSEBACK FROM 3rd-CENTURY TURKEY AND A GROUP OF ODDLY DRESSED BLACK MEN.

see also 70 gezelligheid

A thoroughly Dutch family holiday

Sinterklaas is celebrated in the Netherlands on December 5. It is a thoroughly Dutch family holiday where children are treated to gifts and adults spring surprises and compose humorous poems about each other. At its core is a bishop from 3rd-century Turkey who is buried in Italy, but children believe he lives in Spain.

Walk through the streets of a Dutch town in early December and you are very likely to run across a dignified old fellow with a long white beard, wearing a mitre on his head and a red cape, accompanied by exotically dressed jet-black assistants. You will probably even encounter this unusual group several times and you may even see several such brightly coloured groups at a time.

Is it carnival time? No, but it's definitely a holiday. Sint-Nicolaas (Saint Nicholas), popularly known as Sinterklaas, is the protagonist of the most popular and most Dutch of Dutch holidays. His holiday is celebrated on the eve of the 5th of December, the evening before the holy man's death. Sinterklaas is the ultimate family holiday and it is all about the presents distributed on the saint's behalf.

The presents make it even more of a holiday for shopkeepers. Every year, Dutch households spend an average of 130 euro on Sinterklaas gifts, and this combined with Christmas (December 25-26) and New Year's Eve (December 31) makes December the highlight of the year for merchants.

Young children are firmly convinced that Sinterklaas really does exist. Fearful and trembling, they await what will happen on the holiday evening, because the imposing holy man is good to good children but strict to naughty ones. 'Those who are good get sweets, those who are naughty get the rod', says one of the countless Sinterklaas songs heard continually in homes and schools during this time. According to folklore, the naughtiest are taken away in the burlap sack in which Sinterklaas brings presents. The fact that this never happens is a secret kept with remarkable discipline by adults and older children.

The Sinterklaas mood is in full effect in the weeks before December 5. Festive lighting hangs in the streets and shop windows are full of traditional treats: gingerbread nuts, chocolate initials, speculaas figures, chewy gingerbread and marzipan. One town abstains from this festival: Grouw does not celebrate Sinterklaas, but in February it marks the feast of Saint Peter, who is suspiciously reminiscent of his colleague Nicholas.

The holy man rides over the rooftops on a grey horse.

01 Picture from an old Sinterklaas songbook
02 Zwarte Piet pursuing a naughty boy
03 Sinterklaas arriving in Amsterdam

According to folklore, the saint takes the naughtiest children away in a burlap sack.

Sinterklaas has had tougher competition from Father Christmas. About ten years ago, more and more Dutch people turned to the jovial benefactor from the North Pole who is modelled on Sinterklaas. For a while, it was feared that one of the Netherlands' most beautiful traditions had had its day, but it was not so: in time, most recognised Father Christmas as a third-rate imitator.

For children, the time before Sinterklaas is a feast in itself. They place their shoe by the chimney, leaving a carrot or some hay in it for the saint's horse, and with a little luck they may do this several times. According to tradition, the holy man rides over the rooftops on a grey horse, dropping gifts through the chimney into the shoes. The fact that many modern homes do not have chimneys and shoes are placed near a radiator has not yet fazed a single child.

But there's something in it for adults too, and how! By means of surprises – unusual gifts wrapped in imaginative ways – and the humorous poems included with the presents, they freely make gentle fun of each other. Not all the Dutch are talented poets, of course, but made-to-order rhymes can be ordered on the Internet, honouring and chastising family members, loved ones and even bosses and other superiors for their good and bad sides in a way that is unthinkable in everyday life. The Dutch get things off their chest in the name of Sinterklaas, making a thoroughly Dutch tradition out of the feast of a holy man from Asia. ■

05 Carrot and hay for the saint's horse **07** Every year at the end of November Sinterklaas arrives by boat 'from Spain' **09 & 10** Traditional Sinterklaas sweets: gingerbread nuts, pastry letters and chocolate initials **11** Illustration from the book *St. Nicolas*, written in 1928 by Pierre and Germaine Noury

Who was Sinterklaas?

Around 300 A.D., Saint Nicholas was the bishop of the city of Myra in what is now Turkey. He had a great reputation as a miracle worker, and one such miracle is the basis of his fame as a bringer of gifts for children. But the saint was also quick-tempered: during the Council of Nicaea in the year 325, he ended up behind bars after knocking down the eminent priest Arius of Alexandria with a well-aimed punch. Nicholas' reputation appealed to the imagination in Europe and in the late Middle Ages he was long the most popular saint there. In the 11th century, Italian merchants even brought his bones to Bari.

According to the Dutch tradition of Sinterklaas, the holy man is not from Turkey but from Spain, a country that was long considered the cradle of all things exotic and beautiful. His helper, Zwarte Piet (Black Peter), did not appear until around 1850. He is probably based on exotically dressed servants from the Dutch colonies. When the Netherlands developed more and more into a multicultural society, the black servant became a moral dilemma for the Dutch, but politically correct experiments with white, blue and even multicoloured *Pieten* have been unable to overcome the force of tradition.

Facts The Dutch love raw herring • A typical Dutchman eats an average of 85 kilos of potatoes a year • Exotic food is also popular • When eating out, Dutch people choose exotic food more often than any other nationality • 73 restaurants have one or more Michelin stars

Myth The Netherlands is a country of culinary morons with no good restaurants • The Dutch are crazy about offal, curried rabbit and fish pudding • The potato originates from the Netherlands

Dutch cuisine

MANY FOREIGNERS THINK THE NETHERLANDS IS A CULINARY DESERT, WHERE THE PEOPLE MASH EVERYTHING TOGETHER AND EAT RAW FISH. GOOD RESTAURANTS ARE ALSO SUPPOSEDLY FEW AND FAR BETWEEN.

see also 82 cheese 86 spreads & toppings 88 drop 92 Dutch booze

Dutch delight

The Netherlands is seen as a culinary desert by many foreigners; a country full of people who mash all their food and eat raw fish. Even so, 73 Dutch restaurants are listed in the Michelin 'food bible', and in the better establishments typical Dutch specialities like sprouts mashed with potatoes are the latest trend.

All the criticism aimed at Dutch cuisine suggests that the Netherlands is not the place to go for a culinary holiday. Dutch cuisine is said to be one big hotchpotch. The Dutch like to eat potatoes mashed with vegetables, and soup that is so filling it is a meal in itself. The Dutch mash *all* their food together and are no connoisseurs, as is evident from their love of raw herring and *balkenbrij*.

What on earth is *balkenbrij*? Most Dutch people may have heard of this old-fashioned dish made with offal, blood and fat, but they have never seen it, let alone tasted it.

The Dutch like variation, sometimes eating traditional food and sometimes opting for exotic.

Fables like this are not uncommon in articles on Dutch cooking. To put the record straight, offal, curried rabbit and fish pudding do not appear on the day-to-day menu of a typical Dutch family. It is interesting to see that the names of these dishes are often spelled incorrectly. Perhaps this is a reflection of the accuracy of the culinary research.

However, this does not mean that all the information is incorrect. Dutch people do eat hotchpotch, potatoes mashed with kale, and filling soups. These are popular traditional winter dishes. Raw herring, preferably consumed fresh from the fish van, is another favourite, and is considered a delicacy by many Dutch people.

Contrary to what many people think, the potato does not originate from the Netherlands. This misconception may be due to the famous Van Gogh painting *The Potato Eaters*. The Spanish brought the potato to Europe from South America in the 16th century. It took a long time for this tuber to become the mainstay of

the evening meal in the Netherlands, but once it had captured this position there was no going back. Many Dutch people swear by a classic meal of meat, vegetables and a generous helping of potatoes with gravy.

Even so, this is only one part of Dutch cuisine. Of course, there are still Dutch people who almost have a heart attack when they hear a vegetarian is coming to dinner, and the average annual potato consumption is 85 kilos per capita. However, potato variations like chips and rosti are becoming increasingly common, and rice and pasta have slowly been gaining ground for decades. In addition, different eating habits such as vegetarianism are more common and more accepted in the Netherlands than in neighbouring countries. In fact many Dutch people like experimenting in the kitchen. They devote considerable time and attention

01 Successful integration: tourist consuming a raw herring the classical way **02** Traditional winter dish: hotchpotch with smoked sausage **04** To be found in every Dutch kitchen: the masher

to unusual starters, recently discovered exotic main meals, and imaginative salads. If they don't fancy the famous but rather bland Dutch tomato – known as a 'water bomb' in Germany – they choose tomatoes imported from Spain instead. Dutch supermarkets and other shops have offered an extensive range of domestic and foreign food products for many years, as well as recipe books with dishes from global cuisines. However, even the most experimental amateur chef does not completely reject the traditional Dutch cuisine. A bowl of pea soup or an old-fashioned Dutch meatball with potatoes and sprouts will often be enjoyed in front of the television while one of the immensely popular cookery programmes is being broadcast. The desire for variation seems to be the key rather than a funda-

mental choice for either traditional or experimental. The same attitude can be seen when Dutch people eat out. They want something new, something different. Studies have shown that when eating out Dutch people choose 'exotic' food more often than any other nationality. This explains why over half the restaurants in the Netherlands are foreign. Italian, Chinese and Indonesian restaurants have reshaped the culinary landscape, as these ethnic groups have been in the country for decades (the Indonesians as a result of the Dutch colonial past). Nowadays Afghan, Mongolian, Mexican and Ethiopian restaurants can also be found. All this may leave you wondering whether there are any restaurants that serve traditional Dutch food. Well, these do exist, and their menus include dishes

like herring, marrowfat peas and chuck steak. However, the vast majority of the guests are foreigners, not Dutch people.

What about the quality of these restaurants? Some foreigners can be rather condescending in their comments, but these opinions are not shared by the trend-setting Michelin experts from France. In the 2005 Michelin *Red Guide*, the 'food bible', 64 restaurants have been awarded a coveted Michelin star, seven establishments have two stars and two restaurants even have the maximum three stars. According to Michelin rival GaultMillau, Dutch cuisine can hold its own with the international top.

Michelin predicts that now they have grown up, so to speak, the top Dutch chefs will allow themselves to be increasingly inspired by grandmother's cooking. This tendency can already be observed in some trendy restaurants, where sprouts with mashed potatoes are selling like hot cakes. ■

05 Preparing *poffertjes* (tiny pancakes), a sweet delicacy **08** The hot meatball (*warme bal*) is a popular snack, but also often served at dinner **10** Turkish pizza baker **11** The famous bag of French fries, with or without mayonnaise, is the *raison d'être* of thousands of snackbars **15** *Haagse hopjes*, famous coffee candies from The Hague **22** Doughnut balls are a traditional treat at New Year's eve **26** Popular winter dish: thick pea soup with sliced sausage **27** Preparing mustard according to traditional methods **28** Mussels are farmed in the Oosterschelde, off the coast of Yerseke

Facts The Dutch eat fifteen kilos of cheese per person annually • They were producing cheese even in prehistoric times • The Netherlands is the world's largest exporter of cheese, butter and milk powder • Traditional cheese markets are held in summer in Alkmaar, Edam and Gouda • The Netherlands is also a dessert paradise • A popular Dutch game is known as 'butter, cheese and eggs'

Myths The Dutch are cheeseheads • A 'Frau Antje' is a prostitute who takes payment in cheese

cheese

EVERYWHERE, EVEN IN INNER MONGOLIA, CHARMING, SMILING DUTCH CHEESE-MAIDS ARE DEPLOYED TO RUTHLESSLY FOIST PLATTERS OF CUBED CHEESE ON VISITORS TO TRADE FAIRS AND OTHER EVENTS.

see also ▤ **78** Dutch cuisine   ▤ **86** spreads & toppings   ▤ **94** frugality   ▤ **102** the merchant

A Mecca for cheeseheads

Julius Caesar even wrote about it in his time: the Dutch have something about cheese. And indeed they do. In no other country is the selection as broad or as varied. Cheese with cumin, with cloves and even with nettles – it's not considered unusual in the Netherlands, the world's largest cheese exporter. A real head for cheese.

This reputation for being cheese freaks is not something recent: archaeologists have concluded from excavated pottery that the inhabitants of the Low Countries were making cheese even in prehistoric times. And none other than Julius Caesar described the Dutch habit of consuming cheese, in the 1st century B.C.

At that time, no one had heard of Gouda, and Edam was not on the map either, but now those names are music to the ears of cheese lovers worldwide. Gouda is the most commonly produced variety, but the distinctive round cheeses of Edam are more famous. These are made in a bowl-shaped mould known as a *kaaskop* (cheese head), a word used in Belgium as a disparaging name for the Dutch. Cheeses intended for export are given a striking red coating of paraffin to preserve them.

It is a privilege to live in a Mecca of cheese, but there is also a drawback. Step into one of the countless cheese shops and your senses of taste and smell are assaulted from every direction by a dizzying array of varieties. There are dozens of types of cheese, from what foreigners consider normal 'yellow' cheese to varieties with added flavours, such as Leiden (with cumin), and Frisian clove cheese. There is even nettle cheese, and virtually all varieties are available in different flavours: young, slightly mature, mature, sharp or old, full-fat and reduced-fat, salty, reduced-salt or low-salt, factory cheese or farmer's cheese. The choice is yours.

In the land of the cheeseheads, about 700 millions of the stuff is produced annually. About three quarters of it is exported, making the Netherlands far and away the biggest exporter of cheese in the world.

This proud position is partly the result of intense

01 Husband and wife running a cheese farm in Haastrecht
02 On his way to the cheese market in Edam

> Cheese shops feature a dizzying array of temptations.

promotion. Everywhere, even in Inner Mongolia, charming, smiling Dutch cheese maids are deployed to ruthlessly foist platters of cubed cheese on visitors to trade fairs and other events. The German market was conquered some fifty years ago with a blonde cheese maid in traditional costume. Frau Antje, as she is called in Germany, has had to put up with much over the years, being portrayed as a prostitute and drug addict more than once on magazine covers as a symbol of what some saw as the Netherlands' having gone to ground. But the results of her mission are incontrovertible: every year, in fact, some 200 million kilos of Dutch cheese are sold in Germany.

The Netherlands has had a lasting image as the land of cheese since the 18th century, but the Dutch were certainly exporting cheese hundreds of years before then. A good illustration of how the cheese trade operated in those times can be seen by visiting the cheese market in Alkmaar, where the famous cheese carriers, who formed a guild as early as 1619, still run from spring to autumn. Edam and Gouda also have traditional cheese markets in the summer.

Of course, not all of the billions of litres of milk that flow in the Netherlands each year are used for cheese. The Dutch themselves each drink 66 litres of it annually and the Netherlands is the world's biggest exporter of butter and powdered milk. All around the world, consumers in shops and supermarkets are confronted by images of Dutch cows and farmers' wives on packages and cans.

A large amount of milk also goes into the production of quark, yoghurt and a colourful range of sweet desserts. The Netherlands is a paradise not only of cheese but also of dairy-based desserts. Supermarket shelves

03

The Dutch awoke one day to the *vlaflip*, a combination of yoghurt, vanilla *vla* and lemon syrup.

groan under the weight of a multitude of ice creams and especially *vla*, a type of pudding. There's chocolate, caramel, vanilla, banana, strawberry *vla*, and – we're not making this up – Ajax *vla* in honour of the Amsterdam football club, and this is just a selection from the overwhelming assortment. On the occasion of the Queen's official birthday, shops will even offer special Orange *vla*.

07

The great popularity of dairy products at home is also partly the result of intensive advertising campaigns. Slogans such as *Melk moet!* (Milk is a must) and *Melk, goed voor elk* (Milk is good for everyone) are engraved in the collective memory. For years, a comic-strip character named Joris Driepinter (roughly translating to 'George three pints') convinced the Dutch of the need to consume three glasses of milk daily, and the dairy industry promoted the idea of 'a handful of cheese' as a snack between meals. And in the time that there were not yet dozens of types of *vla*, the

Dutch awoke one day to the *vlaflip*, a combination of yoghurt, vanilla *vla* and lemon syrup, to be assembled by consumers at home, that became a huge success.

11

Being traders through and through, the Dutch know how to market their products. They now produce as much 'Greek' feta as the Greeks themselves, albeit from cows' milk rather than from goats' or sheeps' milk. Exports of the Dutch feta are very successful. The Greeks love it. ∎

15

03 Cheese carriers in action at the famous cheese market in Alkmaar **13** Relief at the old weighhouse for cheese, built in 1668, in Gouda **15** Charming lady, dressed up as a cheese maid at the carnival **16** The cheese market in Gouda **18** The infamous cheese slicer is not a Dutch, but a Norwegian invention

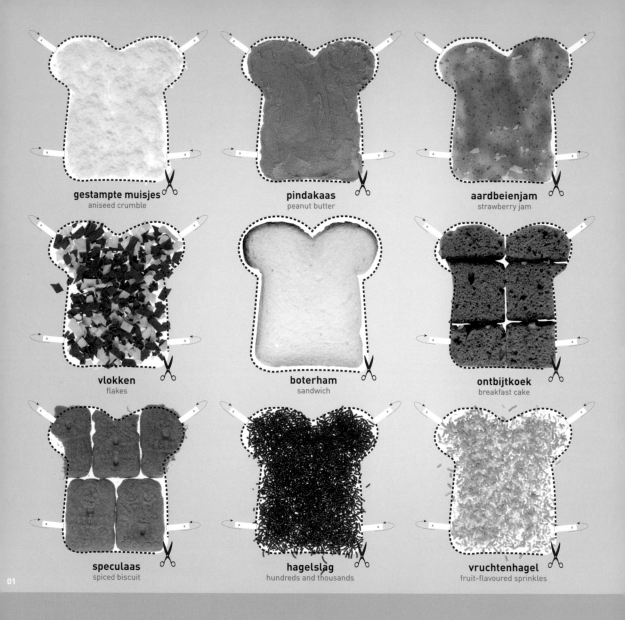

gestampte muisjes
aniseed crumble

pindakaas
peanut butter

aardbeienjam
strawberry jam

vlokken
flakes

boterham
sandwich

ontbijtkoek
breakfast cake

speculaas
spiced biscuit

hagelslag
hundreds and thousands

vruchtenhagel
fruit-flavoured sprinkles

01

spreads & toppings

THE TOURIST WOULD NOT BE ANY MORE SURPRISED TO SEE A GROUP OF ANGRY NATIVES SURROUNDING A CAULDRON CONTAINING HALF A DOZEN EXPLORERS, RATHER THAN A SLICE OF BREAD WITH *HAGELSLAG*.

see also 📖 **78** Dutch cuisine 📖 **82** cheese

The art of decorating bread

Who could be daft enough to eat chocolate on bread? To the incomprehension of just about the entire world, the Dutch spread and sprinkle every imaginable form of candy on their bread. 'You must really love your dentists!'

The unsuspecting tourist sitting down at the Dutch breakfast table is in for a major culture shock. The kind of shock that temporarily fixes the gaze and has the mouth struggling powerlessly for words. Stunned, he looks on as the Dutchman, with a look of contentment on his face, sprinkles a load of chocolate flakes over his slice of bread. The surprise would not be any greater if he was watching a group of angry natives surrounding a cauldron containing half a dozen explorers.

Hagelslag is what the Dutch call the chocolate candy with which they decorate their bread in four main varieties: dark, milk, white and mixed. Similar, but rougher, are the equally varied 'chocolate flakes'. This stuff is just the tip of the sugary iceberg which is so important to the Dutch bread-eating culture.

'Do you Dutch folks love going to the dentist or something?', the tourist asks aloud at the breakfast table. Of course not, comes the reply, we're not stupid! The Dutch eat two bread-based meals a day, so a bit of variety is much needed. This is why there are so many different types of bread, from pale white, through 'tiger bread' and more or less every shade of brown, to the coal-black rye bread and the pride of every self-respecting breakfast table: *ontbijtkoek* (breakfast cake).

Foreigners are more likely to associate sweet Dutch spreads with children's parties than a serious meal. For instance, *muisjes*: a sickly sweet topping in equally sweet colours. You can't put that on your bread, surely? In fact, there is one type of *muisjes* that the Dutch do not eat on bread, but only as a traditional treat. When a child is born, visitors are feted with a *beschuit* (rusk) sprinkled with these round *muisjes*; blue if the baby is a boy and pink in the case of a girl.

What other interesting items have the Dutch come up with for decorating their thin slices of bread? Easily enough for an army of anthropologists to write a weighty dissertation on. For example, take the apple

syrup detested by foreigners, the pungent Dutch peanut butter, or the exotic delicacy known as *kokosbrood* (coconut bread). It goes without saying that there are also many different types of chocolate and hazelnut spreads. A particularly festive topping is the spicy *speculaasjes*, biscuits which were once only eaten around the feast of Saint Nicholas.

The unavoidable question is: are the Dutch allergic to savoury fillings? With its reputation in the dairy industry, and its flourishing bio-industry, the answer

> **Foreigners are more likely to associate sweet Dutch spreads with children's parties than a serious meal.**

could only be negative. Cheese and meat products are popular toppings, as are tomato, cucumber and egg. The combination of the latter three has caused a stir in sandwich bars in the form of a *broodje gezond* (healthy roll), an interesting name considering the quantities of mayonnaise added: enough to plaster a room with. Of course, the advantage of the mayonnaise is that it's easy to sprinkle *hagelslag* on it. ∎

02 When a child is born, the father and mother treat visitors to *beschuit met muisjes*. Pink *muisjes* if the baby is a girl, blue in case of a boy **03** Old bakery in Den Bosch

Drop (liquorice) is the national sweet • The Dutch eat four kilos of liquorice per person per year • Dutch emigrants and expats get their fix over the Internet • The rest of the world finds the black sweets inedible • A tourist who doesn't like *drop* is known as a drop-out *Drop* is the Dutch solution to worldwide overpopulation • *Drop* is known as 'black gold' • Eating too much drop leads to black moods

ZACHT ZOUT G

drop

IF THE DUTCH HAD TO STEAL BIKES TO FINANCE THEIR ADDICTION TO LIQUORICE, NO TRICYCLE WOULD BE SPARED.

The darker side of Holland

The Dutch would kill for it; tourists would rather die than eat it. No sweet is more controversial than the typically Dutch *drop*. The Dutch each put away four kilos of it annually. Tourists smile politely, believing the Dutch to be insane. The Dutch smile back politely, thinking 'Fine, you'll always be a drop-out that way'.

Ask a Dutchman if he has any *drop* on hand and the answer will rarely be no. This jet-black combination of liquorice root extract, gum arabic, sugar and sal ammoniac is the national sweet par excellence and much more popular than other typically Dutch goodies like *stroopwafels*, *speculaas* or *Haagse hopjes*.
The Dutch all agree that the inventor of *drop* deserves a statue on the Dam in Amsterdam, but the identity of that inventor and the time of *drop's* ingenious discovery is unknown. *Drop* was once medicine. Dutch pharmacists were already using the liquorice root centuries ago in syrups and pills for the common cold, but it is unclear when *drop* made its glorious debut in Dutch living rooms as a sweet.
In many homes, the '*drop* tin' or a glass jar full of the stuff is a common feature with its own place on the table or in a cupboard, but in reality it often moves around the house. Family members reach for it while watching television, doing homework, playing games and whatever other excuses they can come up with. The jar usually contains several types of *drop* and picking out the tastiest ones is something of a sport. After a while, only the least favourite type remains and then the accusations fly: 'You always eat the best ones!' The influence of *drop* on family relations and Dutch society should not be underestimated.
There are dozens of types of *drop* and new ones are continually added: sweet, salty, double salt, honey-flavoured, coin-shaped, cat-shaped, liquorice willies, you name it. Supermarkets and other shops sell a range of drop but sweet shops, chemists and stalls at markets are more fun, where *drop* is laid out invitingly in large bins for drooling shoppers to put together their own mixtures with a scoop. These mixtures end up in the jar at home or on the night table, or else they are taken in briefcases and coat pockets to work, where many a desk drawer attests to the Dutch addiction to

02 Traditional shop in the village of Exmorra

In foreign lands, it becomes painfully obvious what the connection to home really is: not skating or the royal family, but *drop*!

drop. Many Dutch travellers also routinely take a large bag of *drop* with them on holiday.
On average, the Dutch eat four kilos of *drop* per person annually and the number of *drop* addicts is alarmingly high. If, like many drug addicts, they had to steal bikes to finance their habit, no tricycle would be spared. The most pitiable are emigrants and expats, deprived of their black gold, far from home.

In foreign lands, it becomes painfully obvious what the connection to home really is: not skating on flooded meadows or the royal family, but *drop*! The Internet has somewhat relieved their suffering as they can now order from online *drop* shops.

There is a good reason that *drop* is available only in small quantities outside the Netherlands: foreigners can't stand the stuff. Tourists view the black sweets offered by Dutch friends with a mixture of mistrust

Tourists view the black sweets with mistrust: 'Are you trying to poison me?'

and disgust. Comments vary from 'Are you trying to poison me?' to 'Time to leave' and a few are convinced that *drop* is a Dutch solution to global overpopulation. Sweets should be sweet and have nice colours, and definitely should not be bitter, salty and black.

The Dutch revel in this undisguised aversion and like to frighten foreigners with a little *drop*. Nonetheless, their judgement is mild: it's something you have to *learn* to eat, they say with the characteristic voice of those who like to guide visitors around their own paradise. You should start eating it as early as possible, so it's not so surprising that tourists are so startled by it. A bit of a shame, though, and a tourist who doesn't like *drop* will always be a drop-out, of course.

The Dutch do realise that such testimonials will do little for worldwide *drop* relations and that no Dutch product is less likely to be a successful export. But their mood is not black, despite their addiction. Perhaps the newest *drop* invention will catch on: the *dropshot*, a drink containing twenty percent alcohol. The idea is that if you throw in enough alcohol, every-one will like the taste.∎

03 Liquorice 04 Confectionery in Hoenderskerke

100 gr. 0 80

muntdrop

coin-shaped liquorice • Lakritzengeld
 èce de monnaie de réglisse • regaliz de moneda
monete di liquirizia • lakritsmynt

100 gr. 0 80

katjesdrop

cat-shaped liquorice • Katzenlakritze
réglisse en forme de chaton • regaliz de gatto
gli abitanti del lago • lakrits atter

100 gr. 0 90

laurierdrop

laurel liquorice • Lorbeerlakritze
réglisse au laurier • regaliz de laurel
liquirizia amara • lakritsblad

100 gr. 0 80

boerderijdrop

farmer-shaped liquorice • Bauernlakritze
astille de réglisse en forme de fermier
la granja • gli abitanti della fattoria

per stuk 0 10

veterdrop

liquorice laces • Schnürsenkellakritze
lacet de réglisse • regaliz de cordón
stringhe di liquirizia • lakritssnören

70 cl 8 59

dropshot

dropshot • Dropshot • dropshot
dropshot • dropshot • dropshot

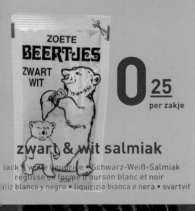

ZOETE
BEERTJES
ZWART
WIT

0 25
per zakje

zwart & wit salmiak

lack & white liquorice • Schwarz-Weiß-Salmiak
réglisse en forme d'ourson blanc et noir
aliz blanco y negro • liquirizia bianca e nera • svartvit

1 15
per mat je

drmdrop

pastille de réglisse à sucer • regaliz de pulgar
liquirizia piatta • lakritsmatta

100 gr. 0 80

zoute drop

salty liquorice • Salzlakritze
pastille de réglisse salée • regaliz salado
liquirizia salata • saltlakrits

100 gr. 0 80

honingdrop

honey liquorice • Honiglakritze
pastille de réglisse au miel • regaliz de miel
liquirizia al miele • honungslakrits

per blikje 4 50

droplulletjes

liquorice willies • Lakritzenpimmel
réglisse en forme de phallus • regaliz de pichita
cazzetti di liquirizia • lakritssnoppar

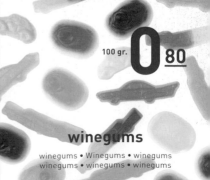

100 gr. 0 80

winegums

winegums • Winegums • winegums
winegums • winegums • winegums

Facts Heineken is one of the five largest breweries in the world • Heineken is also the largest exporter of beer in the world • Dutch beer is drunk in over 170 countries • The Heineken brewery in Zoeterwoude is the largest brewery in Europe • Amsterdam housed the oldest distillery in the world • The English words 'gin' and 'brandy' are derived from the Dutch words jenever and brandewijn

01

02 03 04 05

Dutch booze

THE OLDEST DISTILLERY IN THE WORLD OPENED IN AMSTERDAM IN THE 16th CENTURY, BUT IT WAS SCHIEDAM THAT BECAME FAMOUS FOR ITS GENEVA. AT ONE TIME THE CITY HAD AS MANY AS FOUR HUNDRED DISTILLERIES.

Barley water and firewater

Dutch geneva, widely known as 'gin', was all the rage several centuries ago. Nowadays this intoxicating tipple is seen more as a drink for elderly men, and distillers export more vodka than traditional Dutch 'firewater'. Heineken now has sole responsibility for upholding the Dutch reputation for excellent booze. This sparkling Dutch lager is sold in more than 170 countries.

Heineken is so famous that people sometimes think the name is a synonym for Dutch beer. However, Heineken is not the only Dutch brewer, and it is not the oldest either. Founder Gerard Adriaan Heineken established the company in 1864 after purchasing an Amsterdam brewery that had already been in existence for almost three hundred years.

Heineken is by far the largest brewer in the Netherlands. With an annual turnover of ten billion euros, this beer multinational is one of the five largest breweries and also the largest beer exporter in the world. Its barley water is brewed in no less than fifty countries and is sold in over 170 countries.

The Heineken brewery in Zoeterwoude is the largest in Europe. The brewery in Amsterdam is no longer in operation, but here the popular tourist attraction The Heineken Experience offers anyone interested in beer a peek in the brewer's kitchen.

Heineken not only brews under its own name, but also produces dozens of other brands, including the world-famous Amstel beer. Although the two breweries merged in 1968, Amstel is still made according to the original recipe.

There are many more large and small breweries in the Netherlands, the smaller of which tend to stick to the traditional methods. Beer is also brewed in some Dutch monasteries.

Geneva is every bit as Dutch as Heineken. It is a potent alcoholic corn spirit to which juniper berries are added during the distillation process. The first distillery in the world opened in Amsterdam in the 16th century, but it was Schiedam that earned the reputation of geneva centre. At one time the town had as many as four hundred distilleries in operation. The grain needed to make the geneva was milled in twenty giant mills. Five of these still exist, including the mill De Noord, which is the highest in the world and measures over 44 metres from the ground to the tip of the upper sail.

In addition to geneva, the distillers also made a range of liqueurs. The spice, blossom, fruit and coffee required for these colourful drinks came from all over the world and were imported by the Dutch

Heineken is the largest beer exporter in the world.

East India Company (voc) and the West India Company (wic). These liqueurs are still made and are a highly successful export product.

The situation is slightly different for geneva. This firewater is still made in Schiedam and other places, but the future does not look rosy. Young people prefer to drink cocktails and trendy drinks rather than a tipple favoured by elderly men, and as geneva is not attracting popularity in other countries either, the distillers are seeking alternatives.

One of these is vodka, which is now being produced successfully by several distillers. This drink is exported to dozens of countries. Incidentally, according to an old and unsubstantiated tale, vodka is a Dutch invention. Tsar Peter the Great is said to have taken the drink back to Russia with him after having stayed in Zaandam for a brief period in 1697 to fathom the secrets of Dutch shipbuilding. His investigation was evidently conducted primarily in the local inn. ■

01 The Museum for Beer Advertisements in Breda **03** Geneva glass **04 & 07** The Spirits Museum De Gekroonde Brandersketel in Schiedam is a Mecca for geneva and liqueur lovers, and a working distillery too **06** The art of geneva drinking

SALE

SALE

01

02

Facts The Dutch are frugal and prudent • Banks and insurance companies manage a tidy 200 billion Euros in savings and pension schemes • The Dutch are the most generous charity donors in the world

Myths The Dutch are stingy • The cheese slicer is a Dutch invention

03   04

frugality

TELL ANY MARKET TRADER IN EGYPT THAT YOU ARE FROM THE NETHERLANDS AND CHANCES ARE HE WILL BURST OUT LAUGHING, EXCLAIMING: '*KIJKEN, KIJKEN, NIET KOPEN!*' (LOOK, LOOK, BUT DON'T BUY). IT IS THE ONLY DUTCH SENTENCE HE KNOWS.

Not a penny more!

They give you one biscuit with your coffee, before carefully using their cheese slicer to present you with a near-invisible bit of cheese. Are the Dutch really as stingy as their worldwide reputation suggests? If so, then how come they are also the most generous charity donors in the world?

It is one of the most persistent clichés about the Dutch. They invite you to coffee, offer you one tiny biscuit before closing the lid right in front of your nose. Could they be any less hospitable? Could they be any stingier?

The Dutch find all this quite amusing. Of course, some Dutch people *are* stingy, but there are just as many who are more than happy to share their biscuit barrel with their guests. Besides, as everybody knows, all the scrooges live in The Hague. They will only ever offer you a half-filled cup of coffee. Even though there is not a single witness to this 'fact', the *Haagse bakkie* (Hague cuppa) has become famous throughout the land.

The Dutch nevertheless have a universal reputation for being stingy. Tell any market trader in Egypt that you are from the Netherlands and chances are he will burst out laughing, exclaiming: *'Kijken, kijken, niet kopen!'* (Look, look, but don't buy). It is the only Dutch sentence he knows.

Now, the Dutch do not splash money about, that much is true. They look after the pennies. Why buy something expensive if you can get it cheaply? The company behind the margarine brand Zeeuws Meisje cleverly played on that mentality by using a Zeeland farmer's wife in its television commercials, praising the margarine with the slogan *Geen cent teveel!* (Not a penny more).

This echoes the deep-rooted Protestant virtues of hard work and frugal living. Prudence used to be a bitter necessity for many Dutch citizens. With a bit of luck, they were able to scrape together a little nest egg to protect themselves against unforeseen circumstances, placed in an old sock or under the mattress. Although this is no longer a necessity in these days of prosperity, many Dutch people still save for a rainy day.

Banks and insurance companies manage a tidy 200 billion euros, making the Dutch world champion savers and insurance policyholders.

The frugality of the Dutch is also reflected in the huge popularity of certain practical household tools: the bottle scraper, the Vacuvin and the infamous cheese slicer, to many overseas visitors the ultimate symbol of Dutch frugality. The inventor of an appliance that produces such miserly pieces of cheese must surely have been an incorrigible scrooge.

The Dutch are of course known throughout Europe as inventors and cheesemakers, but inventors of the cheese slicer? No, that is an honour too far. In 1925, this invention was accredited to a furniture maker from the Norwegian town of Lillehammer. The invention was not lost on a people who have turned prudence into an art form.

> **For overseas visitors, the cheese slicer is the ultimate symbol of Dutch prudence.**

So does this prudence actually imply that the Dutch are misers? No, on the contrary. The Dutch are among the first to open their wallet whenever there is a collection on behalf of a charitable cause. Indeed, they head the international list of charity donors. Conservation groups, relief organisations and human rights organisations can always rely on their loyal and generous support. When it comes to charitable causes, the Dutch open their piggy banks not with a cheese slicer, but with an axe. ∎

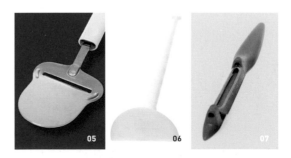

03 Made in Holland: the low-energy light bulb **04** The most famous pig in the Netherlands **05, 06 & 07** Symbols of Dutch frugality: the cheese slicer, the bottle scraper and the parer

01

Facts The VOC was the first multinational in the world • It dominated Asian trade during the 17th and 18th centuries • International trade was the main driving force behind the growth of the Dutch economy, heralding a Golden Age • For over a century, the VOC remained the only contact between Japan and the outside world • The WIC was notorious for its slave trading • The WIC founded New Amsterdam, present-day New York

VOC The Dutch East India Company

IN THE TWO HUNDRED YEARS OF ITS EXISTENCE, OVER FIVE THOUSAND SHIPS OF THE VERENIGDE OOSTINDISCHE COMPAGNIE (THE DUTCH EAST INDIA COMPANY) SAILED TO ASIA. INTERNATIONAL TRADE BROUGHT UNTOLD RICHES TO THE NETHERLANDS.

see also 📖 06 water 📖 100 Flying Dutchman 📖 102 the merchant 📖 106 made in Holland 📖 118 Amsterdam

A sea of success

Situated along the North Sea and in the estuary of three large rivers, the Netherlands is a natural transit port. The Dutch have always had a close relationship with the sea, first as fishermen and then as merchants. International trade brought the country untold riches, thanks mainly to the Dutch East Indian Company, the first multinational in the world.

By the late Middle Ages, the Dutch had become major players in European shipping. They initially traded with England and Italy, before turning their attention to Baltic countries. Eventually, Dutch ships could be found in all the major European ports.

In the late 16th century, Amsterdam merchants became interested in East Asia. The Portuguese were already sourcing their spices from there, making vast profits in the process due to their monopoly position. The Amsterdam merchants sent four ships via Cape of Good Hope to Asia, with the sole aim of finding the naval passage to Indonesia and breaking the Portuguese monopoly.

Two years later, only three ships had returned. Although two-thirds of the crew had perished, the voyage demonstrated that the 'promised land' of East Asia was accessible. Other cities were eager to join in on the adventure. The cash came flooding in. However, there was a flipside to this success: profits plummeted due to fierce mutual competition.

In the 17th and 18th centuries, the port of Amsterdam was 'a forest of masts'.

Therefore, in 1602 six trading companies combined forces to become one entity, the Dutch East India Company (voc). It was granted full and exclusive rights to trade in Asia and was given far-reaching powers by the Dutch government. The company was allowed to enter into agreements with local rulers and, if necessary, to use force. It even deployed its own army.

In the two hundred years of its existence, five thousand voc ships left the Dutch waters in search of riches. From Arabia to China, dozens of trading offices were established, as well as a staging post on the southern tip of Africa, present-day Cape Town.

At the centre of the Asian trade was Batavia, the present-day capital of Indonesia, Jakarta. The city's warehouses were stacked with goods waiting to be shipped to the Netherlands. From here, the voc also coordinated the trade between Asian ports.

The inter-Asian trade was a clever way to source sought-after goods in the absence of any interesting and affordable European products for the Asian market. A small amount of silver bought silk in China,

01 Replica of the voc ship *Amsterdam*, moored in front of the Netherlands Maritime Museum in Amsterdam 02 Naval heroe Michiel de Ruyter. Painting in the Netherlands Maritime Museum 03 Detail of an old house in Medemblik 04 voc products from East India, exhibited in the Netherlands Maritime Museum

which in turn was exchanged for gold and copper in Japan. This was used to purchase textiles in India that were traded for spices from the Moluccan Islands, which were worth their weight in gold back in Europe. This trade network was often maintained by force. The VOC frequently did battle with its European competitors, and the local population was not spared if it dared to obstruct the merchants. The Dutch adopted a heavy-handed approach when it came to maintaining its trade monopoly on nutmeg, mace and cloves. Thousands of people were killed on the Moluccan Banda Islands alone.

Where necessary, the state lent a helping hand. The formidable Dutch war fleet loved nothing better than to teach the enemy of the Dutch merchants a lesson. These battles helped cement the reputation of naval heroes such as Michiel de Ruyter, Maarten and Cornelis Tromp and Piet Hein.

The VOC quickly became the most powerful trading company in the world. At the height of its powers, it employed 25 thousand people, including 11 thousand soldiers. According to one eyewitness account, the port of Amsterdam was 'a forest of masts'. In the two hundred years of its existence, the VOC commissioned the construction of 1500 ships.

International trade brought untold riches to the Netherlands, and the period of 1585 to 1670 became known as the Golden Age. In trading cities such as Amsterdam, canalside houses mushroomed, shaping the monumental character of the city.

In 1621, a second famous trading company was founded, the Dutch West India Company. The company secured a trade monopoly along the west coast of Africa and on America. The WIC earned an unsavoury reputation due to its involvement in the slave trade. There were however also positive reports from the areas overseen by the company. The progressive work of governor Johan Maurits of Nassau in Brazil

is still regarded as a milestone in Brazil's history. The foundation of New Amsterdam is another high point in the company's history. The WIC founded the city in 1625 after purchasing the island of Manahatta from the American Indian population. In 1664, governor Peter Stuyvesant transferred ownership of the colony, home to eight thousand Dutch residents, to the English. The city was renamed New York.

Barring a few exceptions, the driving force behind the activities of these companies, which would result in a longlived Dutch dominance over the Dutch East Indies, Surinam and the Dutch Antilles, was not colonial motives, but commercial ones. 'Converting the heathens' was also an alien concept to the merchants. It is mainly for this reason that Japan granted the VOC permission to continue trading, while it refused entry to other European countries. For over a century, the VOC remained the only contact between Japan and the outside world.

Lack of money, mismanagement and a change in economic and political circumstances led in 1799 to the bankruptcy of the VOC. It was an inglorious end. However, all over the world, from the Barents Sea to Brooklyn and from Wall Street to Tasmania, names, forts and other relics remind us of this illustrious period of Dutch history.■

05 Building a replica of the VOC ship *De Zeven Provinciën* [The Seven Provinces] in Lelystad **06** Reconstructed octant. The heavily damaged original was found in the wreck of the *Hollandia*, built in 1742 **07** Detail of an old house in Hoorn **08** Old headstone for a sailor in Hollum on the island of Ameland **09** Inside the VOC ship *Amsterdam* **10** The country estate of Trompenburgh in 's-Graveland, dating from 1680 and built by Admiral Cornelis Tromp **11** VOC café in the *Schreierstoren* [Weeper's tower] in Amsterdam, where sailors used to say goodbye to their loved ones **13** Gate of a 17th century country estate along the river Vecht, where rich merchants built many beautiful country houses **15** Replica of the VOC ship *Batavia* in Lelystad **16** Detail of a house at the Zaanse Schans, near Zaandam

Facts The Flying Dutchman was the terror of all seamen who were to round the Cape of Good Hope • The legend became particularly well-known through Wagner's opera *Der fliegende Holländer* • Tennis star Tom Okker was nicknamed *The Flying Dutchman* abroad • KLM is still known by this name • There is a monument to the ghost ship in Terneuzen

Myths The Flying Dutchman really exists

01

Flying Dutchman

THE TERRIFYING CAPTAIN STOOD AT THE RAILING, WHITE AS A GHOST, RAIL-THIN, HIS LONG BEARD FLAPPING IN THE WIND. WOE BETIDE THOSE WHO SAW THE GHOST SHIP, FOR THEY KNEW THEIR LAST HOUR WAS AT HAND.

see also 96 VOC

The spectre of the seven seas

It was the terror of seamen who had to round the Cape of Good Hope: an encounter with the Flying Dutchman. Those who saw the ghost ship and its dead crew knew that their last hour was at hand. The story behind a ghostly legend.

Ask the Dutch about The Flying Dutchman and their thoughts will turn to KLM rather than a ghost ship. After it was founded in 1919, the national airline proudly added the name The Flying Dutchman to the fuselage of its aircraft. Some may think of Tom Okker, the agile tennis player who sometimes appeared to fly across the court and who was nicked The Flying Dutchman abroad. Most Dutch people have no more than a vague idea of the legend of the ghost ship.

And yet the story totally fits the Netherlands' famed history of navigation and trade. It takes place in the 'Golden' 17th century and begins in the port city of Terneuzen in the province of Zeeland, from which captain Van Straaten bravely sets sail for the East Indies on the orders of the Dutch East India Company. The journey is uneventful to the southern tip of Africa, but Van Straaten's ship encounters heavy weather at the notorious Cape of Good Hope. For months he attempts to round the Cape, battling against the current and an intense storm, to the despair of his crew. The helmsman mutinies but is unceremoniously thrown overboard, along with his Bible, by Van Straaten. The skipper vows to continue his attempts until the end of time, even if the devil himself has to help him.

He really ought not to have done that. The storm intensifies, the sails are torn to shreds and a loud curse is heard from the heavens: the ship is doomed to roam the oceans for all eternity.

The helmsman is unceremoniously thrown overboard along with his Bible.

The spectre of the ship and its dead crew travelling into the storm under full sail became the terror of all seamen who were to round the Cape. The terrifying Van Straaten stood at the railing, white as a ghost, rail-thin, staring into an indeterminate distance, his long beard flapping in the wind. Woe betide those who saw the ghost ship, for they knew their last hour was at hand.

There are different versions of the story, which was first put in writing in the 19th century. The captain, for example, is also known as Van der Decken and, in Germany, as Von Falkenberg. The legend became widely known because of Richard Wagner, who wrote the opera *Der fliegende Holländer* in the mid-19th century. Thanks to the composer, we are able to listen to the legend in the safety of our own homes, leafing casually through the different versions of the story. Sightings of the ghost ship are not reported anymore. Those who require a tangible reminder would therefore do well to travel to Terneuzen rather than to the Cape, as the story of the ghost ship and its deranged captain is kept alive in the form of a monument in Van Straaten's home port. ∎

01 Comic *De Vliegende Hollander*, written and illustrated by Jack Staller, published by Arboris
03 & 04 KLM, the oldest airline in the world still operating, boasted in its infant years the advertising slogan 'The Flying Dutchman: Once a legend, now a reality'. In modern times The Flying Dutchman was replaced by a flying swan

Facts The Netherlands is a leading trade and transport centre • The country is home to many European distribution centres. Many leading multinationals have based their European headquarters in the Netherlands as well • The port of Rotterdam is the second biggest port in the world, after Shanghai • The port employs some 60 thousand people and 350 million tons of goods are transhipped each year • Amsterdam is the largest cocoa port in the world • Schiphol airport serves forty million passengers a year and processes 1.3 million tons of freight

01

the merchant

THE PORT OF ROTTERDAM IS A SYMBOL OF THE ECONOMIC PROSPERITY OF THE NETHERLANDS. THE PORT EMPLOYS SOME 60 THOUSAND PEOPLE, AND TRANSHIPS 350 MILLION TONS OF GOODS A YEAR.

see also 06 water 96 VOC 114 Rotterdam 118 Amsterdam

The eternal transporter

The contemporary Dutch businessman has more in common with the successful 17th century merchant than he may think. He is enterprising, matter-of-fact and keenly focused on overseas markets. To a large extent, the Dutch are still a nation of transporters.

At the end of the Golden Age, the Dutch economy had slowed down dramatically. This was due mainly to the fact that, by the 18th century, an increasing number of countries had begun transporting their own goods. This posed a significant budget challenge for the Dutch, who had traded mainly in overseas goods and did not have a domestic industry to speak of. They specialised primarily in processing commercial products. This lack of versatility meant that the Netherlands was soon overtaken by England, the cradle of the Industrial Revolution. Industrialisation also helped the German and Belgian economies grow more rapidly than the Dutch. Holland did not become a fully-fledged industrialised nation until the late 19th century.

It took until the end of the Second World War for the Netherlands to become one of the world's richest countries again. Following in Germany's footsteps, the country experienced rapid economic growth. The Netherlands went high-tech. However, the lack of natural resources – with the exception of natural gas, which makes a healthy contribution to the treasury – makes it heavily dependent on other countries. Furthermore, the relatively small domestic market has forced big industrial enterprises to focus their attention on the international market. To this day, there is a strong correlation between industry, distribution and transport.

As in the 17th century, this small country is a high-powered trade and transport centre. The fact that an impressive number of European distribution centres and foreign multinationals have set up their headquarters in the Netherlands speaks volumes.

The reputation of the Netherlands as a major distribution channel is also demonstrated by its contribution to European inland shipping and freight haulage. To strengthen and consolidate this reputation, it is vitally important that the country maintains and improves its infrastructure. Over the past decades, the Dutch government has invested billions of euros in improving and extending its rail network.

The high-speed rail line planned for 2007 will connect Schiphol airport to Rotterdam, the Belgian capital of Brussels and the French high-speed rail network. A 160-kilometre freight line running from the port of Rotterdam to the German border will also be put into operation in 2007. The

01 & 03 The port of Rotterdam 04 The flower auction Flora in Rijnsburg 05 Schiphol airport, home to 'Flying Dutchman' KLM

new line guarantees a fast transit of goods from the port of Rotterdam to the European hinterland, strengthening the competitive position of the port.

The port of Rotterdam is a symbol of the economic prosperity of the Netherlands. The port employs some 60 thousand people and indirectly 310 thousand people make a living thanks to the port. Each year, over 350 million tons of goods are transhipped, mostly overseas.

For years, Rotterdam held the title of world's biggest seaport city. Until 2004 that is, when it was overtaken by Shanghai. This doesn't bother Rotterdam in the least. The Chinese seaport city is not a direct rival. What is more important is that the Port of Rotterdam remains the biggest seaport in Europe.

Over the past decades, the Dutch government has invested billions of euros in extending its railway network.

Amsterdam also boasts an impressive port. Although overshadowed by the port of Rotterdam, Amsterdam makes not only the list of Top Ten European port cities, but also the Top 25 of the world. Amsterdam is the largest cocoa port in the world and is also a major cruise port. The port employs 38 thousand peole, indirectly even some 85 thousand.

Ships en-route to Amsterdam pass the famous waterworks at IJmuiden: the North Sea sluices are the world's largest sea sluices and see fifty thousand ships pass through each year.

Let the residents of Rotterdam boast about their port; Amsterdam has its very own showpiece: Schiphol is one of the biggest and best airports in the world, and is a major global player in the carriage of passengers

and freight. Each year, Schiphol serves forty million passengers and processes 1.3 million tons of freight. However, with over 400 thousand aircraft movements a year, Schiphol is unable to extend without causing major disruption. A plan is therefore being considered to create a second mega airport on an island in the North Sea.

Schiphol is home to KLM, Royal Dutch Airlines, the oldest operating airline company in the world. The airline, which in its infant years boasted the advertising slogan 'The Flying Dutchman – Once a legend, now a reality', merged with Air France in 2004. This came as a bit of a shock to ardent KLM supporters, whose loyalty to the company borders on mild nationalism. Was this the end of the 'blue giant'? Could it continue operating under the wings of its big French brother?

KLM managers have little time for sentimentality. With characteristic rationality, the Dutch giant realised that the future of aviation rests in the hands of a small number of strong alliances. Companies that fail to find a safe haven will almost inevitably be doomed to failure. A merger was the only way to prevent the Flying Dutchman from becoming a legendary has-been in the not-too-distant future. ∎

06 Iron ore storage near the Rotterdam port **08** Construction of the second Heinenoord tunnel underneath the Maas **12 & 15** Hothouse cultivation in Bleiswijk. The surrounding area, the Westland, is the largest greenhouse farming area in the world. Vegetables, fruit and flowers, mainly for export, are grown in the 'glass city' **13** Modern shopping centre in Utrecht **14** The river Waal near Tiel. Dutch ships play a prominent role in the European inland shipping sector **17** Man walking on his glasshouse in Moerkapelle, demonstrating how high the water would rise without protection from dunes and dykes. The area is far below sea level

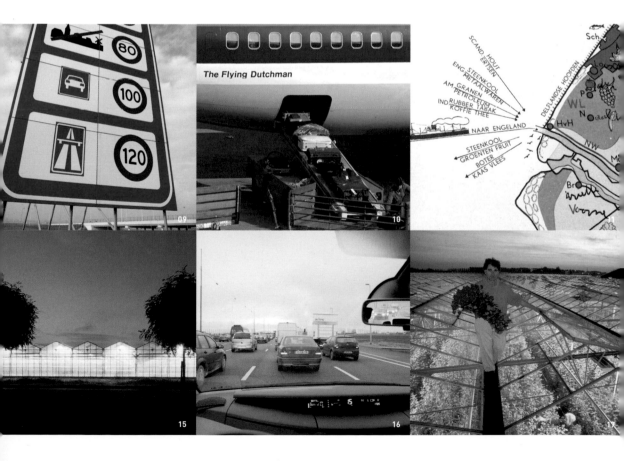

Facts Compared with other countries, the Netherlands is simply brimming with inventors • Dutch business is noted for its innovative performance • Over ten thousand inventions can be attributed to the Dutch electronics company Philips • The first Dutch aeroplane was built by aviation pioneer Anthony Fokker

made in Holland

THE PHILIPS COMPANY BOOM BEGAN IN 1898 WITH AN ORDER FROM THE RUSSIAN TSAR FOR FIFTY THOUSAND LIGHT BULBS. APPARENTLY THE COMPANY'S REPUTATION ABROAD WAS EXCELLENT EVEN THEN.

   see also 📄 **96** VOC 📄 **102** the merchant

Land of inventors

What do microscopes, fire engines and binoculars have in common? They are all Dutch inventions dating from the 17th century. While Dutch merchants were abroad trading in nutmeg and pepper, much inventing and producing was going on at home. And it still is today.

Holland, land of inventors. Nowhere in the world are as many ideas born, plans developed, prototypes constructed and patents requested as in the Netherlands. Strangely enough, the cheese slicer, that miracle of ingenuity and thrift, escaped the attention of Dutch inventors. The credit for that must go to a Norwegian. Nevertheless, the Dutch have more than made up for that one error. Holland's inventors bombard the world community with plans both brilliant and otherwise. When it comes to innovation, Dutch business has a reputation to maintain. The Eindhoven based truck company Daf, which once surprised the world with its Continuously Variable Transmission (cvt), or in Dutch *het pientere pookje* (the clever stick), excels with nifty inventions that have improved the truck driver's life considerably. The multinational Shell has invested substantially in research into clean energy. And the multinational Unilever, which produces foodstuffs and home and personal care products, has developed a low-fat margarine and various other dairy products that help reduce high cholesterol levels. The claim is so conclusive that the Dutch Heart Foundation is recommending the products, and a leading health insurer is reimbursing clients who buy these products with up to forty euros a year.

But the greatest inventor of them all is surely the Eindhoven-based electronics company Philips. Since Gerard Philips shone that first light bulb in 1891, and founded a company that would provide the world with

Philips wanted to shed its lights upon the world with more than just lamps

reliable and affordable lighting, the company has not only grown into a multinational with 165 thousand employees in over sixty countries, but also has a list of inventions to its name that easily surpasses the ten thousand mark.

The company's boom began in 1898 with an order from the Russian Tsar for fifty thousand light bulbs. Apparently the company's reputation abroad was excellent even then, as it still is today. Philips is responsible for lighting the Great Pyramid of Cheops, the Golden Gate Bridge, and the famous New Year's Eve party at Times Square in New York.

But Philips wanted to shed its light upon the world with more than just lamps. In 1928 it demonstrated a television set, twenty years prior to the introduction of television in the Netherlands. From the 1930s

02, 03 & 04 From dynamo to compact disk: Philips is a shining example of the Dutch inventiveness

onwards, the company did a lot of research into radio and radio tubes. In the 1950s, work was carried out in an area of great importance to the Dutch people: the development of a bicycle light driven by a dynamo. The same principle was applied to the classic razor known as the Philishave. The most famous inventions in the history of Philips are probably the audio cassette recorder, the video cassette system, and the compact disc. The company surprised coffee drinkers in 2001 with the Senseo, a coffee machine using coffee pads. The machine, which was developed in cooperation with the Douwe Egberts coffee company, became a huge success.

Since 1928, the company has also been producing medical systems, including x-ray equipment that has made it possible to treat tuberculosis effectively. The importance of this sector grew with the increasing average life expectancy. In 2002, a defibrillator was developed for home use, and two years later a highly-praised scanner. Philips Medical Systems is one of the world's largest producers of medical equipment. Another monument to innovation was the Dutch aviation company Fokker, which went bankrupt in 1996 and underwent a partial merger with the Stork Aerospace company. Fokker's founder, Anthony Fokker, was an aviation pioneer, as was KLM's founder Albert Plesman. Fokker built the first Dutch plane, the Spin

The Fokker F27 Friendship, which was launched in 1958, became known as a real 'workhorse' and is still widely used.

(Spider). The plane designer and builder became world famous with his Fokker F27 Friendship, the best selling propeller plane ever. The plane, which was launched in 1958, became known as a real 'workhorse' and is still widely used.

In 1969 Fokker produced his first jet plane, the F28 Fellowship. The ultra-modern Fokker 50 and Fokker 100, successors to the F27 and F28, came onto the market in the 1980s. These were to be the last planes developed by the famous company. Heavy competition combined with the 1990s aircraft industry crisis and the unstable dollar, were to mean the end for this most innovative of aircraft builders. In 1996, Fokker folded its wings. ∎

05 Commemoration for Gerard Philips, founder of the Philips company: 'At this place Gerard Philips produced the first Philips light bulb' **06** The Senseo coffee machine **07** Anthony Fokker, founder of the aviation company Fokker **08** Old poster for the Philips radio

PHILIPS RADIO

01

flower power

FAMOUS FOOTBALLERS RUUD GULLIT, MARCO VAN BASTEN AND FRANK RIJKAARD, WHO MADE MAJOR CONTRIBUTIONS TO THE SUCCESS OF AC MILAN IN THE 1980s AND '90s, WERE KNOWN IN ITALY AS THE *TULIPANI*, OR 'TULIPS'.

see also 📄 **36** orderliness 📄 **102** the merchant

The world's biggest flower stall

The cultivation of flowers and flowering bulbs has been elevated to an art in the Netherlands. Most flowers sold worldwide come from the narrow strip of land along the North Sea. The Netherlands is especially known as the land of the tulip, although the plant is not of Dutch origin. Not that the Dutch care about that – the passion for flowers has deep roots.

To illustrate this, let's first travel back in time to a 17th-century house along an Amsterdam canal. We see a wealthy merchant in a chair, staring in devotion – not at the new floral wallpaper but at a vase of flowers. The vase does not resemble the ones we know now: it has holes in it from each of which a flower protrudes, unique in type and colour. A mixed bouquet, if we can call it that, was the height of 17th-century flower appreciation.

Since then, a passion for flowers has been a part of Dutch culture. For many Dutch people a home is uninhabitable unless there is at least one bunch of flowers on the table, and many do not rest until their gardens are a riot of colour in spring and summer. When visiting, the Dutch are in the habit of bringing a bouquet of flowers, and not just on formal occasions such as birthdays: flowers are customary at other, more casual times as well. The Dutch say it with flowers, as the advertising slogan puts it.

Countless florists' shops are essential to cultivating this addiction to flowers. There are even special flower markets, the most famous of which is in Amsterdam, although the one in Utrecht has the best atmosphere.

Even more than in the living room, the blossoming flower culture is seen in cultivation and trade the domain of the merchant who is also a lover of flowers. The ornamental flower trade is an industry worth billions in which tens of thousands of Dutch people earn a living. Most products are destined for export. Some five billion euro is earned in flower and plant exports alone each year. The majority of flowers sold worldwide come from the Netherlands.

The centre of this business is the enormous Aalsmeer flower auction, the largest flower auction and also the largest covered commercial building in the world.

Every day in this dynamic city of flowers, nineteen million flowers and two million plants from seven thousand growers change hands. About eighty per cent of sales is sent abroad.

More interesting for tourists, however, are the famous bulb fields. Flowering bulbs have been grown in the Netherlands since the late 16th century. The fields cover 25 thousand hectares and when in bloom, they form a gigantic multicoloured mosaic. The most commonly grown flowers are tulips, hyacinths, narcissi, lilies and gladioli. To the dismay of tourists, the flowers are mechanically lopped off before they are in full bloom, a process that strengthens the bulbs.

01 & 02 Callantsoog, working in the tulip fields

For many Dutch people, a home is uninhabitable unless there is at least one bunch of flowers on the table.

The most important bulb regions are the area north of Alkmaar and the area south of Haarlem. The latter is home to the Keukenhof, the world's largest flower garden, which draws three quarters of a million visitors each spring. It is then that the *bloemencorso* takes place, a carnivalesque tradition in which a pro-

cession of floats travels from Haarlem to Noordwijk, laden with exuberant floral creations incorporating one and a half million hyacinths alone. Such parades are also held in other parts of the country throughout the year.

All in all, it is not surprising that around the world, the Netherlands is associated with flowers, and especially with tulips, a symbol of everything Dutch. Famous footballers Ruud Gullit, Marco van Basten and Frank Rijkaard, who made a major contribution to the success of AC Milan in the 1980s and '90s, were known as the *tulipani* (tulips). Businesses are keen to exploit the familiarity of the Netherlands as the land

of tulips, as shown by Tulip Computers and Golden Tulip, an international hotel chain.

But in a sense, the Dutch are flaunting the charms of others, because the tulip is not an indigenous plant: it was imported from the Ottoman Empire (Turkey) in the 16th century. Even the word *tulp* (tulip), derived from the Turkish *tülbend* (turban), is imported. Incidentally, the Dutch immediately cultivated a variety of new types from the imported flower, and Dutch tulips were much appreciated in Turkey in the 17th century. In the Netherlands, the tulip was a true status symbol and the subject of a lively trade. Bulb trading resulted in excessive speculation circa 1637, in which many citizens lost their entire fortunes. Rare bulbs were worth as much as an Amsterdam canal house. One of the victims was the famous painter Jan van Goyen. The teacher of Jan Steen and Paulus Potter, among others, died penniless. Today, the Dutch are not subject to such risk, because nowhere else are flowers more affordable than in the world's largest flower stall. ■

05, 09 & 13 The Keukenhof in Lisse, the world's largest flower garden **06, 08 & 22** Working in the bulb fields in Warmond and Sint Maartensvlotbrug **10** A float bearing the golden coach made of flowers at the annual *bloemencorso*

Facts Rotterdam is the most modern and dynamic city in the Netherlands • The city is a Mecca for lovers of modern architecture • It is home to 600 thousand people, and the second largest port in the world, after Shanghai • The port employs some 60 thousand people and tranships over 350 million tons of goods a year

Myths Rotterdam is a bleak city with no character • Rotterdam residents have no sense of humour

01

Rotterdam

THIS MODERN, EVER-CHANGING CITY IS ALSO KNOWN AS 'MANHATTAN ON THE MAAS'. ASK ANY CITIZEN OF ROTTERDAM TO NAME THE BUILDING HE IS LOOKING AT, AND HE'LL SAY: 'NO IDEA, IT WASN'T THERE YESTERDAY'.

see also 42 architecture 102 the merchant

Deeds, not words

Created around a dam in a small river, Rotterdam grew to become the second city in the Netherlands. It has risen like a phoenix from the ashes after being flattened during the Second World War. Rotterdam is the most modern and dynamic city in the Netherlands and has the second biggest port in the world. From fishing village to Manhattan on the Maas.

Rotterdam actually acquired its character as a dynamic forward-moving city in the 13th century, when a dam was constructed near a small fishing village along the river Rotte. From these humble beginnings, Rotterdam simply grew and grew. A port was established in the 16th century, and it took the village less than fifty years to overtake its neighbour Dordrecht, the oldest city in the county of Holland, to become the second biggest city in the Netherlands.

The port's development, inextricably linked to the development of the city, was spurred on by the separation of Belgium from the Netherlands in 1830. The completion of the Nieuwe Waterweg in 1872 was another important step in the city's progress towards creating an international seaport. The port now stretches across the full length of this eighteen kilometre long connection to the North Sea, and has even been extended into the sea.

The port employs some 60 thousand people. Each year, over 350 million tons of goods are transhipped. For years, Rotterdam held the title of world's biggest sea-port city. Until 2004 that is, when it was overtaken by Shanghai. This doesn't bother Rotterdam in the least. The Chinese seaport city is not a direct rival. What is more important is that Rotterdam remains the biggest seaport in Europe.

The German aerial bombardments of May 1940 mark the blackest period in the history of Rotterdam. Virtually the entire city centre was destroyed, and the port sustained huge damage. The dramatic events are symbolised by the moving sculpture *De Verwoeste Stad* (The Destroyed City) by Ossip Zadkine, depicting a desperate man whose heart has been ripped out of his body. It is better known to locals as *Jan Gat* (John Hole), characterising the wry sense of humour of the city's residents.

Brimming with ambition, the citizens of Rotterdam set to work rebuilding their city after the war

With incredible perseverance, the citizens of Rotterdam turned necessity into virtue after the war. Brimming with ambition, they set to work rebuilding their city, drawing up new plans and expanding the city. They continue to do so to this day. The motto of Rotterdam is *Aanpakken* (Let's work), echoing the sentiments expressed in the song of the famous football

01 The Harbour Museum. In the background the three so-called Boompjes towers, built in 1988 by Henk Klunder **02** In the harbour **03** The Hotel New York, housed in the former head office of the Holland America Line **04** The Erasmus bridge, also known as The Swan, designed by Ben van Berkel and completed in 1996

club Feyenoord: *Geen woorden, maar daden* (Deeds, not words).

This modern city is home to 600 thousand people. Its dynamic character is best reflected by a timeless joke: ask any Rotterdam citizen to name the building on the other side of the road, and he is likely to reply: 'No idea, it wasn't there yesterday'.

Rotterdam has a world-wide reputation of being the centre of modern architecture, never afraid to experiment. The many spectacular, sky-high buildings have earned Rotterdam the nickname of Manhattan on the Maas. It should come as no big surprise to find that the city is home to the Netherlands Architecture Institute, located in an eye-catching building, boasting a sizeable library and temporary exhibitions on all aspects of architecture.

Another eye-catcher is the 808-metre long Erasmus bridge, named after the city's most famous son, the humanist Desiderius Erasmus, born in 1469. The bridge, with its 139-metre tall pylon, connects the city centre to the so-called Kop van Zuid, the 'second city centre' on the site of the former dock areas.

One monument that is literally difficult to overlook is the Euromast, erected in record time in 1960 and raised ten years later to 185 metres. The cube-shaped houses along the Blaak are also world famous. Of the many other internationally acclaimed buildings, the *Kunsthal* (Art hall), designed by the Rotterdam-born architect Rem Koolhaas, deserves a special mention.

Rotterdam also boasts a handful of beautiful old buildings that managed to escape the ravages of the Second World War. Examples include the charming Delfshaven, the old port of Delft which was annexed by Rotterdam in the 19th century. Particularly popular are the 17th century Schieland house, site of the city's historical museum, the graceful Hotel New York, housed in the former head office of the Holland-Amerika Lijn (Holland America Line), and the Van Nelle factory of 1931, a beautiful example of the avant-garde architectural style known as the *Nieuwe Bouwen* (New Building).

Rotterdam is also a haven for culture addicts, with its highly acclaimed art museum Boijmans Van Beuningen and annual events such as the International Film Festival. The city also offers plenty of entertainment, a varied nightlife scene and restaurants and cafés with views of passing ships.

Despite all these accolades, the city has a reputation in the rest of the country for being bleak and bereft of any character. This image harks back to the days when Rotterdam was struggling to liberate itself from the desolation and despair of the Second World War, an image that should be confined to the dustbin of history. The citizens of Rotterdam are welcoming and warm-hearted, and the city itself is brimming with character. The only problem is that it is developing so fast, that anyone visiting the city after an absence of many years will think he has stepped aboard the wrong train.■

05 & 12 The Old Harbour **06** The work of art *Beukelsblauw* **08** Cubic apartments **09** The Dutch version of the monopoly game, starring Rotterdam **10** Train station Blaak **11** The restaurant Zochers **13** Arcade under the Netherlands Architecture Institute **14** The Hef bridge **Detailed information and credits, see back flap**

Facts Amsterdam is the official capital of the Netherlands, but not the seat of government • With a population of 715 thousand, Amsterdam is the largest city in the country • Amsterdam was the trade centre of the world in the 17th century • The famous canals and merchant houses and the paintings by renowned Dutch masters like Rembrandt and Vermeer also date from this period

Myth Coffee is the speciality of the Amsterdam coffee shops • An 'Amsterdammertje' is a small resident of the city

01

Amsterdam

**AMSTERDAM IS A UNIQUE CITY THAT BREATHES FREEDOM AND TOLERANCE.
NO ONE HAS TO KEEP UP APPEARANCES HERE, AS EVERYONE IS EQUAL.
THE SPIRIT OF LIBERALISM SEEMS TO HAVE FOUND A HOME HERE.**

see also 📖 **16** canals 📖 **66** Dutch masters 📖 **96** VOC 📖 **122** Anne Frank 📖 **124** tolerance 📖 **132** Johan Cruijff

Free port for the spirit

Amsterdam is a trade city in heart and soul, with a characteristic atmosphere and a liberal nature. The city is famous for its canals, merchant houses, coffee shops and open prostitution. Amsterdam is very permissive, but it also has plenty to offer in the way of culture and architecture. Although the capital city of the Netherlands is relatively small, it is unrivalled in its cosmopolitan character.

What springs to the minds of people planning a visit to Amsterdam? Of course, all visitors want to see the monumental city centre with its canals and merchant houses. Other attractions include the Rijksmuseum (National Museum), which features works by famous 17th century painters like Rembrandt and Vermeer, and the Van Gogh Museum and the Anne Frank House. Most tourists have heard of the Red Light District, the Wallen, where prostitutes display their charms behind 'shop' windows. Another well-known fact is that you can

buy soft drugs in Amsterdam without worrying about spending an extended holiday in a Dutch prison cell. After the visit, the logical question is whether the city has lived up to expectations. The answer is invariably positive. Amsterdam amply satisfies all requirements. The visitors are thrilled by the museums, deeply moved by the Anne Frank House, awed by the monumental canalside houses and impressed by the extensive network of canals. With a total length of one hundred kilometres, this is the longest canal system in the world, and it cannot be explored with just a boat trip and a city stroll. Visitors to the city are also amazed to see how prostitution flourishes openly against a background of canals and dignified merchant houses. The giggling crowds of tourists who file uninterruptedly past windows bathed

01 Laughter at the Prinsengracht **02** The Oude Schans and the Montelbaans tower **03** City of islands **06** Sailing ships, moored at the Zandhoek **07** The Amsterdam coat of arms

In the narrow streets you can roam endlessly past hidden monuments and traditional and exotic bars, restaurants and shops.

in red light are an attraction in themselves. Not to mention the numerous coffee shops, where different sorts of hash and grass are on display like sweets in a sweetshop.

Everyone agrees that Amsterdam is an exceptional city. This is not just due to the appealing combination of the more standard attractions. Another peculiarity of the city is that, although it is the largest city in the Netherlands, all attractions are within cycling distance. Another striking feature for a capital city is the absence of government buildings – these are all situated in the far more respectable city of The Hague.

The urban hustle and bustle is also exciting: the trams with their nervous jingling bells, the hoards of cyclists, the colourful collection of eccentric characters from all corners of the globe, the markets where all languages of the world are spoken and where dealers tell jokes about the illustrious Jewish pair Sam and Mose, the houseboats carelessly moored in the canals, the thousands of anti-parking posts (*Amsterdammertjes*) that make parking in the city centre impossible, the narrow streets where you can roam endlessly past hidden monuments and both traditional and exotic bars, restaurants and shops, distracted only by a group of Hare Krishna followers banging their drums. Amsterdam is a unique city that exudes an atmosphere of openness and tolerance. No one has to keep up appearances here, as everyone is equal, regardless of ethnic background or religion. The spirit of liberalism, the creed of live and let live, seems to have found a home here. Despite its relatively small size small (715 thousand residents), Amsterdam is a metropolis of great stature.

The marked cosmopolitan character of the city took shape mainly in the period when Rembrandt and Vermeer were producing their famous paintings. In the 17th

century the small country of the Netherlands dominated global trade, and Amsterdam was the prosperous trade centre of the world. During this period, known as the Golden Age, the most important canals were dug and many of the dignified merchant houses and warehouses were built that now shape the character of the city. These buildings with their famous gable ends reveal the status of the merchants, but at the same time the lack of ostentatious adornment reflects their rather sober lifestyle, in keeping with good Protestant custom.

Amsterdam also acquired its reputation for hospitality and tolerance during this period. In the late 16th century, large numbers of Spanish and Portuguese Jews found a safe haven in the city. In contrast with the even larger influx of Jews from Central Europe in the latter part of the 17th century, they made a significant contribution to the welfare of the city. The same applied to the Huguenots (French Protestants), who fled to Amsterdam in large numbers in 1685 or thereabouts. In 1700, besides London, Paris and Naples, Amsterdam was the only European city with more than 200 thousand residents, almost half of whom were foreigners.

The city has never lost this spirit of freedom and tolerance. In the 1960s and '70s, Amsterdam became the hippie capital of the world and the spiritual centre for a hopeful new age – an age of love and peace, propagated in the city itself by none other than Beatle John Lennon. Young people from all corners of the world flocked to Amsterdam, where they smoked pot, made love and contemplated the new idealism. They slept in Vondel Park, named after the famous 17th century poet Joost van den Vondel, and on Dam Square in the heart of the city, which marks the spot of the dam in the Amstel river that gave the city its name in the 13th century. Hippies no longer sleep on Dam Square and Amsterdam is no longer the rich seaport of bygone days, but the character of the spiritual free port remains, ensuring that all strangers feel at home. ∎

10 Café Dantzig 11 Vermeer scene at Madame Tussauds 12 The ship-like Museum New Metropolis, designed by Renzo Piano and completed in 1997 13 The Brouwersgracht 18 The Red Light District

Anne Frank

ANNE WROTE IN HER DIARY THAT SHE INTENDED TO PUBLISH HER NOTES AFTER THE WAR. SHE WANTED TO BE A FAMOUS WRITER, BUT DOUBTED HER ABILITIES.

see also 📖118 Amsterdam 📖124 tolerance

An eternal diary

Her diary is the most translated Dutch book ever and she herself is the symbol of the Holocaust. Anne Frank was fifteen when her hiding place was betrayed. It now attracts nearly one million visitors a year.

The famous *achterhuis* (back house or annex) is now a museum. It is also an indictment of practices so horrible that they defy all comprehension, and a reminder of a lively girl who had her whole life ahead of her.
Anne was born in June 1929 in Germany. Four years later, the Frank family moved to Amsterdam, into which Hitler's troops marched in May 1940.
In July 1942, the family went into hiding with friends in the small back part of the house. There were eight people living there. The front part housed her father Otto's spice business. Some of the employees knew about the people in hiding and supported them. A rotating bookcase connected the two houses.
Anne described her impressions and feelings in a diary that she wrote faithfully for two years. Her words were addressed to an imaginary friend named Kitty. One thing she wrote was that she was planning to publish the diary. She wanted to become a famous writer, but doubted she was good enough. On 5 April 1944, she wrote: 'I know that I can write. Some stories are good, my descriptions of the back house are humorous, much of my diary is expressive, but... whether I really am talented remains to be seen.'
In the meantime she had begun to transcribe the diary onto loose pages. It was supposed to become a novel with the title *Het Achterhuis*.
But it would never be finished. The people in hiding were betrayed in early August 1944 and taken to concentration camps in the Netherlands and Germany. She shared the fate of most Amsterdam Jews. In 1940, the city had 86 thousand Jewish inhabitants. Only 13 thousand of them survived the Holocaust.
Otto Frank was the only one of the eight in hiding to return alive. On returning home, he read the diaries and other texts and decided to comply with Anne's wish to publish them. He edited the texts himself and in 1947 *Het Achterhuis* was published.

01 & 06 Excerpts from Anne's diary **02** The rotating bookcase which formed the entrance to the *achterhuis* **05** Statue of Anne at the St. Janskerkhof in Utrecht

> '**What I still like best of all is that I can at least write down what I think and feel, otherwise I would just choke.**'
>
> Anne Frank in her diary, 16 March 1944

In 1960 the hiding place on Prinsengracht in Amsterdam became a museum, the Anne Frank House. It is one of the most visited places in Amsterdam. Every year, nearly one million people come to see the place where the symbol of the Holocaust was in hiding. The house is empty nowadays, except for a part which is not open to the public. After the war most of the furniture was removed and Otto Frank insisted the house remained that way. Apart from that, the house appears exactly as in Anne's time. The museum also contains exhibitions on racism, anti-Semitism and modern developments.
Anne's diary has been translated into more than sixty languages. Over 25 million copies have been sold worldwide. Anne's wish to become a famous writer came true posthumously. ∎

01

tolerance

**SEVENTEENTH-CENTURY MERCHANTS ALREADY KNEW THAT TOLERANCE WAS
USEFUL. TRADE FLOURISHES ONLY IN A CLIMATE OF FREEDOM AND RESPECT,
AND EVERY CLIENT IS AN INDIVIDUAL, REGARDLESS OF COLOUR OR CREED.**

see also ▤ **11** polder model ▤ **118** Amsterdam ▤ **122** Anne Frank

The liberal society

The Netherlands is known for its tolerance. The country was frequently a haven for refugees facing persecution in their own countries, and the principle that everyone has the same rights is legally established. In many respects the Netherlands is more liberal than most other countries, making the country an earthly paradise for some, a modern Sodom and Gomorrah for others.

01 Famous tattoo shop in the Red Light District in Amsterdam
03 Coffee shop interior 04 *Nederwiet* leaf

The Netherlands has a long tradition of tolerance. The Dutch are accustomed to respecting others' individuality and seeking compromises in the event of conflicting opinions and interests. They are bridge-builders, literally and figuratively, and they readily accept the fact this attitude requires them to adjust as well. Such characteristics are vitally important in a densely populated country, but they are rooted in its trading past and the communal struggle against water.

The threat of water taught the Dutch early on to submit to the common interest, as it was only with a combined effort that they could successfully defeat the danger. Being practical sorts, 17th-century merchants also saw that tolerance was useful. Trade flourishes only in a climate of freedom and mutual respect, and every customer is an individual, regardless of colour or political or religious convictions.

The idea of 'live and let live' is firmly entrenched in the Netherlands, so much so that in the first half of the 20th century, Dutch society became divided into four segments ('pillars'), each with its own philosophy: Catholic, Protestant, socialist and liberal. The pillars had their own political parties, unions, schools, broadcast corporations, newspapers and hospitals, leading many Dutch people to live almost entirely within their own worlds. Under the influence of increasing secularisation, emancipation and prosperity, this unique system quickly became less important from the 1950s on, but remnants are still clearly visible, such as in education and the fragmented broadcasting system.

> **In addition to the unsurpassed local cannabis variety *Nederwiet*, the menus in coffee shops offer at least five or so types of marijuana and hash.**

The Netherlands is known internationally as a country where everyone has a great degree of freedom. Reference is often made to relatively progressive laws on euthanasia and equal rights for homosexuals, openly practised prostitution and the famous policy of tolerance: practices that are legally prohibited are sometimes 'tolerated' as long as they do not result in excessive nuisance, in which case the reins are tightened.

A good example of this is street prostitution, which especially involves drug addicts. Street prostitution is prohibited but is difficult to combat in practice. The decision has therefore been made to tolerate it in remote areas. Quite a few towns saw the creation of *tippelzones*,

where prostitutes can pick up clients, and of gloomy 'working areas' where they can meet each other. This prevents nuisance in various parts of the city and has the added advantage that the prostitutes are less at risk of violence.

A major attraction involving tolerance is the coffee shop. Not because of the quality of the coffee, but because of the soft drugs that are freely sold to customers over eighteen years of age. In addition to the unsurpassed local cannabis variety *Nederwiet*, the menus offer at least five or so types of marijuana and hash. A tour of coffee shops is a must for tourists, and quite a few of them already begin to hallucinate at the very idea of being allowed to order a space cake.

Some incorrectly conclude from this that the Netherlands is a true drug paradise. Only the sale of soft drugs is tolerated, once again on the principle that a complete ban would not eliminate sales, but would make the problem invisible and create more problems. There is no tolerance policy for hard drugs and even the supply of large quantities of soft drugs is not permitted. The question of how coffee shops acquire their merchandise is left unanswered for the sake of convenience. This is one reason that the intricacies of the tolerance policy are difficult to explain to outsiders.

Abroad, the liberal tradition is cause for admiration as well as abhorrence. In the latter case, the Netherlands is portrayed as a modern Sodom and Gomorrah, a country without moral awareness where no rule applies.

Tolerance is also a frequent topic of conversation in the Netherlands itself. National discussions on whether the country is tolerant enough, or perhaps too tolerant, are not unusual. These discussions are not always meaningful, but the fact that they can be held says much about the Dutch climate of freedom. ∎

05 Freedom of opinion: 'Fuck the government' **06** Peace demonstration **07** The Gay Parade passes along the canals of Amsterdam **09 & 14** The Red Light District in Amsterdam **12** Display in a piercing shop **15** The traditional Dutch cheese maid as many foreigners see her

👍 **Facts** The Netherlands is known as a tolerant country • It has a long tradition of tolerance • The principle of equality is entrenched in the constitution • Prostitution in designated 'work areas' and the sale of soft drugs in coffee shops are examples of tolerance policies

👎 **Myths** A *tippelzone* is a jogging track

15

Facts Football is the most popular sport in the Netherlands • The Netherlands' Football Association has over one million members • Dutch football is renowned for its daring, attacking style and tactics • Ajax is the most successful club • Feyenoord and PSV are the other leading clubs • The national team has been World Cup runner-up twice and European Champion once

01

football

THE REPUTATION OF THE NETHERLANDS AS A FOOTBALLING NATION WAS ASSURED FOLLOWING THE 1974 WORLD CUP, WHEN THE NATIONAL TEAM SURPRISED THE WORLD WITH ITS 'TOTAL FOOTBALL'.

see also 132 Johan Cruijff

'Aanvalluuuuh!'

Dutch football enjoys a strong reputation. This is due mainly to the successes of Ajax and the Dutch national team and the daring, attacking style of football. 'Total football', the penalty syndrome and the *Superboeren*: welcome to the Mickey Mouse League.

'Aanvalluuuuh!' (Go for it!)
This primal scream, emitted from the throats of tens of thousands of football supporters, continues to echo around the stadiums. It is usually preceded by a trumpet signal, used traditionally to herald a cavalry charge. A sea of supporters dressed in orange make their voices heard. On the football field, the Dutch play as if their lives depend on it.
And to a certain extent, their lives *do* depend on it. After all, Dutch fans are the most vocal of critics; no nation has such high expectations as the Dutch. The team must win, of course, but winning alone is not

German stadiums were filled with banners bearing the legend 'Granny, we've found your bike'.

enough. We want to see attacking, daring and artistic football, with lots of action from speedy wingers and defenders pushing forward, with players who can play the ball with one touch. The team needs to swing, come on! This style of football is not the exclusive reserve of the Dutch national team; it also helped Ajax create a furore around the world. The disappointment of losing a game is nothing compared to the criticism when the actual performance on the pitch fails to meet expectations.
Dutch football supporters are spoiled. They compare today's performances with the golden years, when Dutch clubs and the national team celebrated their biggest successes. They conveniently forget that there have been worse teams and less succesful periods, too. After all there are the laws of football. To this day, the yardstick is the 'mighty Ajax' of the early 1970s, the team that won three successive European Cups. Possibly even more important, however, is that this team introduced the world to a radical and

tactical concept, which was to enter the history books as the trademark symbol of Dutch football. During the 1974 World Cup, the Dutch national team stole the show with its 'total football', yet needlessly lost to hosts West Germany in the finals. Although the Dutch were inconsolable, the stature of the recently deceased manager Rinus 'General' Michels ('Football is War'), captain Johan Cruijff and Dutch football was cemented forever. Four years later, the team lost the World Cup final again, this time in and against Argentina, but this was a blow that was less hard to take.
It was only in 1988 that the hangover was cured, when the Dutch beat hosts West Germany in the semi-finals of the European Championship and went on to win the tournament. Rinus Michels was once again the manager, but this time the stars on the pitch were Marco van Basten, Ruud Gullit and Ronald Koeman.
The Dutch victory was heralded as a 'second liberation day'. During the tournament, there were references aplenty to the Second World War, including banners sporting the legend 'Granny, we've found your bike', a reference to the mass confiscation of bikes during the German occupation. German drivers and their cars ran the risk of being caught up in the crowds of singing and dancing Dutch supporters, while a huge banner

01 The Orange legion of fans includes big chief 'Orange Feather'
02 Collectors item, 1960s

bearing the text 'You are now in the country of European Champions' was suspended across a motorway near the German border.

Since then, relations between the two arch rivals have vastly improved. And since then, Dutch football supporters have been waiting for the next big success. Victory has been well within their grasp on numerous occasions, but every time they lost the penalty shoot-out. It was the birth of a new trauma. The 'penalty syndrome' became a major headache for players and supporters alike. The nightmare was to last until 2004.

The 'total football' concept has not been widely copied overseas. It is an attractive but difficult system, which makes big demands on the disciplinary skills of all players. Most countries are interested only in the result, not the beauty of the game. As a result, few nations have embraced the concept.

In the Netherlands the system is consistently honoured by Ajax, the leading and most successful club in the Low Countries. Ten international cups – including two world club championships – stand proud in the Amsterdam trophy cabinet, six more than arch rival Feyenoord can boast about, the Rotterdam-based club with its loyal 'legion of fans' who fill the stadium even when times are tough. The contrast between the two clubs could hardly be greater. Ajax is the club of technique, brashness and self-awareness, while Feyenoord supporters believe in hard work and *Geen woorden maar daden'* (Deeds, not words).

The Dutch football league, rather mockingly referred to as the Mickey Mouse League by more affluent neighbouring footballing nations, has a third top club: PSV, sponsored by the multinational Philips. Although the Eindhoven-based club has 'only' managed to win two international cups, PSV have been Dutch champions on many occasions. But when it comes to the crunch, PSV regularly suffered from what is commonly referred to as the 'provincial syndrome', a disproportionately big respect for the 'real' big teams. This syndrome is suffered by a host of other clubs. PSV supporters try to ward off the complex by referring to themselves as *Boeren* (Farmers), while supporters of the relatively insignificant club De Graafschap even go so far as to call themselves *Superboeren*.

With fourteen more clubs in the Eredivisie (Premier League), it is clear that Dutch football is more than just a Mickey Mouse League. And all these clubs have one thing in common: they all want to attack. *'Aanvalluuuuh!'* ∎

08 The Sport Museum in Lelystad **09, 10 & 13** The Amsterdam ArenA, designed by S. Soeters and R. Schuurman, home of Ajax **12** The Ajax Museum

Johan Cruijff's footballing career spanned 704 games • He scored 392 goals • In 1969 he recorded the song 'Oei oei oei (dat was me weer een loei)' • Motto: 'Football isn't football unless the players and the crowd are having fun • Cruijff's statement 'Da's dus logisch' can be found on Delft Blue tiles • All proceeds from the sale of these tiles go to the Johan Cruijff Foundation

Johan Cruijff is not the best footballer of all time

Johan Cruijff

CRUIJFF BROUGHT DEFENDERS TO THEIR KNEES WITH HIS SUBLIME DRIBBLING TECHNIQUES, TURNED PASSING THE BALL WITH THE OUTSIDE OF THE FOOT INTO AN ART FORM AND WAS BLESSED WITH A SUPERIOR FOOTBALLING BRAIN.

The Saviour

Hendrik Johannes Cruijff, nicknamed *The Phenomenon* and *The Saviour*, is regarded by many as the best footballer of all time. The former Ajax player is in any case the most famous Dutchman in the world. He nowadays steals the show with his virtuoso use of language.

Johan Cruijff – not entirely coincidentally blessed with the initials JC – was born in the Amsterdam suburb of Betondorp in 1947. At the age of 17, he made his footballing debut with the Ajax first team, the same team with which he was to win three successive European Cups and many other trophies. The slenderly-built striker quickly made a name for himself. He was fast, elegant and two-footed, he scored beautiful goals, brought defenders to their knees with his sublime dribbling techniques, and turned passing the ball with the outside of the foot into an art form. His superior footballing brain made him a born leader.

Cruijff was one of the first footballers to make a dream transfer. For a huge fee, he moved to Barcelona where he was nicknamed *El Salvador* (The Saviour). Barcelona fans worshipped the ground he walked on. He also played in the United States and at the Spanish club Levante before returning to Ajax, sporting the by now legendary number 14 shirt. He ended his footballing career with arch rivals Feyenoord, promptly helping them become league champions. He earned 48 caps for the Netherlands.

As a manager, Cruijff was a keen advocate of spectacular, attacking football.

Johan Cruijff is regarded by many as the best footballer of all time. The only other contenders are Pele of Brazil and Maradona of Argentina. In Europe, he was voted footballer of the century.

Johan Cruijff has also had much success as a manager. Every inch an *Ajacied*, he managed Ajax and Barcelona, where he advocated spectacular, attacking football. To the frustration of many, he never took up the challenge of managing the Dutch national team.

Since ending his footballing career, Cruijff has been at the helm of his very own training institute, where top sportsmen and women are taught the intricacies of taking up managerial positions in the world of sport. He has also set up the Johan Cruijff Foundation, which champions sports and game projects for underprivileged children around the world.

Cruijff also keeps himself busy writing articles and making regular television appearances as a football analyst. His impressive footballing knowledge and strong opinions make him the ideal football pundit. Although he no longer commands attention on the playing field, he still has an immense influence on the Dutch game.∎

01 The Ajax Museum **02** An altar voor JC in De Bilt **03** Emblem commemorating the best footballer of all times, containing the colours of Ajax (including the legendary number 14) and Barcelona, the two clubs where Cruijff became a craze

Cruijffisms

As a football analyst, Cruijff regularly stirs audiences with his striking use of language. His commentaries have become as legendary as his footballing skills. His quip that *'Elk nadeel hep ze voordeel'* (Every downside has its upside) has permeated everyday speech, and his slip of the tongue *'Hun verdediging was een geitenkaas'* (Their defence was a goat's cheese) has an undisputed timeless quality.

Cruijff regularly bamboozles audiences with little pearls of wisdom that at first glance appear completely nonsensical. 'The Italians can't beat you, but you can lose to the Italians' is another Cruijffian classic. And his 'Football is simple, but there's nothing harder than playing simple football' also gives food for thought.

The *Cruijffisms* have a wonderfully persuasive quality thanks to the matter-of-fact way in which he adds *'Da's dus logisch'* (So that's logical). And should the audience ever think that the great Johan Cruijff has slipped up, he pre-empts their sniggers with this simple motto: 'Before I make a mistake, I won't'.

Facts The Netherlands is a nation of ice-skaters • Competitive skating is dominated by Dutch skaters • Indoor ice rink Thialf in Heerenveen in Friesland is the national skating temple • The *Elfstedentocht* (Eleven Cities Tour) is the largest skating spectacle in the world • Dutch inventors lead the way in competitive skating innovations

Myths The clap skate is a Dutch invention • 'IJspret' is an ice-cream coupe with three different flavours and a dash of banana liqueur

ice-skating

CLUTCHING A KITCHEN CHAIR FOR BALANCE ON THE SLIPPERY SURFACE, DUTCH TODDLERS TAKE THEIR FIRST CLUMSY STEPS TOWARDS A POSSIBLE FUTURE CAREER IN COMPETITIVE SKATING.

see also 📄 20 climate 📄 138 Holland sport

The national passion

When Jack Frost turns the land of water into a land of ice, it is time for the Dutch to get their skates on. Nowhere in the world are people as passionate about skating as in the Low Countries. It is therefore no surprise that Dutch skaters win so many medals at international events. However, this sacred national custom is first and foremost simply an enjoyable pastime.

IJspret (Ice fun) is what Dutch people call their antics on the thin blades. This passion for skating is almost an addiction. The first suggestion of frost is enough to get the entire country sharpening their skates, and as soon as a thin layer of ice appears on the water the daredevils rush excitedly to the nearest pond or canal. Not everyone takes heed of the meteorologists, who warn about the deceptive relationship between wind speed and ice thickness, and every year the enthusiasm of reckless skaters is dampened quite literally by a cold dip.

But once winter really takes hold, there is no stopping the fun. Skaters invade frozen ponds, lakes, canals, waterways, or wherever ice can be found. Skating tours and contests are organised all over the country. The first person to organise a competition on natural ice or on a flooded meadow is a local hero. No one minds getting cold feet.

The impressive distances travelled over the ice by experienced skaters are a reminder of a time in which skating was a necessity rather than a hobby. When the waterways froze up, skating was the fastest and most practical means of getting from one place to another, and in the country special clogs with blades were created by traditional clog makers. The wearers of these primitive skates would be green with envy if they could see the state-of-the-art equipment used by today's professional skaters. They would also be amazed at all the other facilities available to skaters, such as the refreshment stalls that spring up next to the ice in winter, where frozen limbs can be revitalised with pea soup, sausages, hot chocolate, and the notorious Frisian herb liqueur. However, one thing that primitive and modern skaters have in common is that they probably all took their first tottering steps on the ice leaning on a kitchen chair.

01 Ice fun at the Prinsengracht in Amsterdam 02 The thousands of skaters taking part in the Eleven Cities Tour are received as heroes in the cities

The Eleven Cities Tour

It is five o'clock in the morning on a bitterly cold winter's day. Millions of Dutch people settle down excitedly in front of the television. At the same time another million compatriots are braving the cold, slipping and sliding over the frozen waters of Friesland, laden with orange flags, banners and musical instruments. Has everyone gone mad in the Netherlands?

Well, yes, they have gone a bit mad. The Eleven Cities Tour is about to start in Leeuwarden. This is a two-hundred-kilometre skating tour that passes through eleven cities in the Dutch province of Friesland. The tour only takes place in very severe winters – with fifteen tours since 1909 – and it generates unparalleled excitement. The country is gripped with the skating bug for days in advance. Will the Great Tour go ahead or not? Televisions screens are filled with meteorologists giving their opinion, and the Frisian 'section managers' explain in intricate detail what the ice looks like in their section of the route, where the wind may have caused weak spots in the ice, where an 'ice transplant' may be needed, and where *kluning* (walking over the embankment on skates) is unavoidable.

The Great Tour is also a great national festival. The participants are urged on in the eleven cities by German orchestras and crowds of people dressed in orange. With the exception of the elite competitive racers – usually friendly, very powerful country people who earn a living as farmers – most skaters have the Olympic philosophy that taking part is more important than winning. This is a good thing, too, as many thousands do not make the finish, beaten along the way by exhaustion and the brutal conditions. The Eleven Cities Tour is a unique spectacle, providing heroism and tragedy in equal measures.

Once the ice finally takes over from the water, there is no stopping the skaters, who invade every square metre of ice in the country.

Ice-skating as a sport has been dominated by the Dutch for many years. The male skaters have been particularly successful, and they often return proudly from European and world championships weighed down by all their medals. Competitive skating has developed rapidly from an activity for robust amateurs braving snowstorms on outdoor rinks to a professional sport that is practised primarily indoors. The rival professional teams call the shots, and Dutch inventors lead the way in the development of devices aimed at improving times by hundredths of a second. They first came up with aerodynamic skating suits, and these were followed by strips that could be attached to the suit to reduce air resistance. Even more revolutionary was the introduction of

the so-called clap skate, which caused all existing records to be pulverised. Incidentally, the idea for the clap skate had already been suggested by a Canadian one hundred years previously.

The centre of Dutch competitive skating is the indoor ice rink Thialf, which is in Heerenveen in the province of Friesland. Thialf is appropriately referred to as the temple of skating. After all, skating is and will continue to be a sacred national custom. With an orchestra to provide entertainment during the mopping breaks and faithful supporters in exuberant orange costumes, Thialf stays loyal to this deadly serious tradition with a carnival atmosphere. ∎

03 The famous windmills at Kinderdijk form a romantic backdrop for a handful of skaters **04** Top-class skaters Erben Wennemars and Mark Tuitert greeting the audience in the temple of skating, Thialf **07, 09, 11, 15 & 18** World Cup games at the indoor ice rink Thialf **08 & 17** Refreshment stalls spring up along skating tracks **12** Skating on an Amsterdam canal **13** Statue of the Eleven Cities Tour skater in Leeuwarden, Friesland **16** Ice sailing on the IJssel Lake near Monnickendam **19** Skating on the Museumplein in Amsterdam

Facts Although it is a small country, the Netherlands always wins a surprisingly large number of medals at the Olympics • Fanny Blankers-Koen of the Netherlands is the Female Athlete of the Century • The Netherlands is a leader in international korfball • It has won five out of six world championships • Kaatsen and skûtsjesilen are popular Frisian sports

Myths Ditch-jumping is an Olympic event • The Netherlands is home to a sport known as 'mixed showering'

01

Holland sport

FANNY BLANKERS-KOEN WON FOUR GOLD MEDALS AT THE 1948 OLYMPIC GAMES AND WENT DOWN IN HISTORY AS 'THE FLYING HOUSE-WIFE'. IN 1999, SHE WAS NAMED THE FEMALE ATHLETE OF THE CENTURY.

see also 📖 128 football   📖 134 ice-skating

The Flying Housewife and other success stories

Football and ice-skating are not the only sports in which the Dutch do well. Even though it is a small country, the Netherlands consistently obtains a high medal ranking at the Olympic Games. Fanny Blankers-Koen, the Flying Housewife, was even named Female Athlete of the Century.

Blankers-Koen, who died in 2004, excelled at the 1948 Olympic Games in London, winning four gold medals, all in athletic events. Being world record-holder, she was also favoured to win the long jump, but the competition schedule made it impossible for her to take part in the event. She entered the history books as The Flying Housewife and was named Female Athlete of the Century by the International Athletic Federation.

Blankers-Koen was by no means the only Dutch athlete to win Olympic gold in the 20th century, but most success was achieved in water sports such as swimming and rowing, as well as team sports like field hockey and volleyball. The Netherlands is also consistently among the top performers in draughts, although that is not an Olympic sport.

There is one sport in which the Netherlands has been the champion since time immemorial: korfball.

Korfball? Yes, korfball.

It is a sport that distantly resembles basketball, but the goal is not a ring and a net but a basket attached to a pole. The sport was introduced in 1902 by a teacher from Amsterdam and is considered typically Dutch, but this is questionable. The teacher became acquainted with a similar sport in Sweden that was based on an American variation on basketball for women.

What is certain is that the teacher developed the sport further and set out the rules, and that the Netherlands is the undisputed number one korfball nation. Its korfball association is the world's biggest, with a hundred thousand members. Moreover, the Netherlands has won five of the six world championships held to date. Neighbouring Belgium is the primary competitor and the sport is practised in forty countries.

Korfball is a demanding, dynamic sport, but it has a frumpy image to contend with. Yet it is the most emancipated of all sports – each team consists of four men and four women, so it's a mixed sport, which is something the korfball association exploits to revamp its fusty image. A playful campaign emphasised 'mixed showering', wisely omitting to state whether men and women really did step into the showers together after matches.

> A playful campaign
> by the korfball association
> emphasised 'mixed showering'.

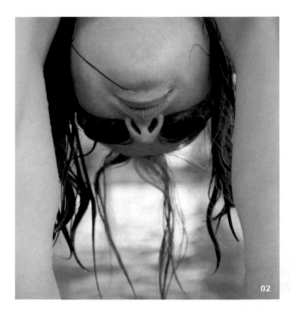

01 Although ditch-jumping is not a big sport, the participants rise to a great height

Modern trends in korfball are not the least bit frumpy. It is now played on artificial turf (it is incidentally both an indoor and an outdoor sport) and it is steadily becoming more professional. A recent revolutionary change has been the introduction of a yellow plastic basket to replace the one traditionally made of rattan, which had the drawback of becoming crooked over time. The yellow 'factory basket' supposedly also

Urban golf involves a course running through a city. Players traverse the streets while playing.

makes the game faster and more telegenic as a ball striking the basket will bounce far onto the field. Possibly even more Dutch than korfball is the sport of *kaatsen*. The term 'Dutch' is actually not apt here, as *kaatsen* is a Frisian sport that is virtually confined to the province of Friesland. The game is played by teams of three players and it is halfway between baseball and tennis, albeit without rackets or bats.

Kaatsen is all done with the hand. Competition games and championships draw many viewers in Friesland. Equally Frisian is *skûtsjesilen* – sailing races involving *skûtsjes*, which used to carry cargo on Frisian waterways. These ships with their trademark brown sails now compete every summer in spectacular races on the IJssel Lake and the Frisian lakes, drawing hundreds of thousands of spectators around the country.

Of course, there are many sports in the Netherlands that are purely recreational and which do not draw huge crowds. A typically Dutch pastime is *slootje-springen*, or ditch-jumping using a vaulting pole.

The trick is to reach the other side without getting wet and the fun part is that it is certain that not all participants will have mastered the trick. The unlucky jumper hanging from the pole that is stuck in the mud, waiting for the inevitable dunking, is a figure of fun and a source of amusement.

Boerengolf (Farmers' golf) is the somewhat curious name for a rising sport that is a variation on ordinary golf, which is gaining in popularity in the Netherlands. *Boerengolf* is played not on a well-tended golf course but in a meadow. A large ball is used to keep track of things easily and a stick with a wooden shoe attached to it is used instead of a club. The holes are replaced by buckets set into the ground.

Another variation on golf is *stadsgolf* or 'urban golf', which involves a course running through a city. Players traverse the streets while playing and can at least count on many curious onlookers, but whether this sport will achieve eternal fame is open to doubt. ∎

04 Rising sticks in the meadow: farmer's golf is a rising sport 05 A new plastic korfball basket 11 Annette Roozen is one of many disabled sporters in the Netherlands. She holds the world record on the hundred metres sprint: 17.20 seconds 12 *Skûtsjes* with their characteristic dark sails on a Frisian lake

Facts The Dutch are world champion recyclers and waste separators • The Dutch also excel at collecting coupons • the Netherlands has the highest concentration of museums of any country in the world • Second-hand shops are the country's least well-known tourist attraction
Myths Thrift and prudence are outmoded concepts

01

collecting

THE ATTIC, JAMMED PACKED WITH JUNK, REVEALS THE CENTURIES-OLD HOARDING TRADITION OF THE DUTCH IN ALL ITS GLORY.

see also 🗋 36 orderliness 🗋 94 frugality

The Great Collector

The Dutch are keen collectors. The Netherlands has the highest concentration of museums of any country in the world. Anyone scouring the street market on *Koninginnedag* can put together a complete living room for next to nothing.

01 Alarm clock museum in Meijel 02 Collection of footstoves in the church of Midden-Beemster 03 Grandmothers' kitchen museum, a private collection kitchenware in Wedde 04 The Dutch are passionate stamp collectors

Wie wat bewaart, die heeft wat (Waste not want not), is a cherished expression in the Low Countries. This popular saying is a throwback to a distant time, when a person's fate was determined by unpredictable circumstances, not knowing from one day to the next whether there would be enough to live on. Old objects were not thrown away if they still served a useful purpose. Even the smallest items were squirreled away, as they might come in useful one day. Prudence and thrift were essential virtues.

Although most Dutch people have now lived in relative prosperity for several decades, the hoarding mania has not subsided. It may take a few more generations to 'adjust the genes' to this change in circumstances. Throwing things away is still seen as 'wasteful'. Coupled with a keen environmental awareness, this deep-rooted conviction has turned the average Dutch citizen into a passionate recycler. They are world champion recyclers and waste separators, and will even separate their old batteries and chemical waste.

That same hoarding frenzy has earned them a second accolade: that of world champion coupon savers. Country-wide, kitchen drawers bulge with trading stamps and discount vouchers, promising the proud owner special discounts or freebies. The petrol giant Shell discovered just how deep-rooted this hoarding passion was when the company decided to stop issuing its popular trading stamps, believing it to be an outmoded way to secure customer loyalty. National outrage and an impending boycott of Shell petrol stations was the result. To the Dutch, saving and hoarding are an 'acquired right'.

Most companies have a healthier attitude to this philosophy of prudence. Under the heading *Hamster-weken* (Hoarding weeks) the biggest supermarket chain in the Netherlands, Albert Heijn, encourages consumers to purchase goods in bulk. This comparison with the hamster, the little rodent that stocks up on provisions, failed to offend anybody. On the contrary, a glimpse into the average Dutch larder or cellar confirms the success of such campaigns. The Dutch seem perpetually prepared for rough times; to this day, nothing is left to chance.

It is however not in the cellar, but in the attic that the national hoarding frenzy is revealed in all its glory. The attic, jammed packed with junk, symbolises the centuries-old hoarding tradition of the Dutch. They are renowned for hoarding just about everything. The renting of storage space has become a booming business. Television programmes featuring homeowners keen to root through their old junk in the hope of finding hidden treasures have become a runaway success.

Once a year, on *Koninginnedag*, padlocked storage boxes

The Dutch seem to have succeeded in preserving their entire heritage for the next generation.

are opened and the contents of countless attics are put up for sale for next to nothing. Unregulated street markets are the favourite hunting terrain for that other passionate hoarder: the collector. Although collecting appears to have lost some ground as a national hobby, the collector is not quite on the list of endangered species. Specialist fairs and theme stores are flourishing, and the Internet is becoming an increasingly popular arena for a diverse group of collectors looking to sell and buy their cherished possessions.

The Netherlands is awash with a mind-boggling variety of impressive collections, owned by or entrusted to private individuals, foundations, companies, governments and of course museums. The country has at least 1200 museums, the highest concentration of museums of any country in the world. As well as being home to some of the most famous museums in the world, with their impressive architecture and professional organisational structures, the Netherlands has a wealth of small museums, often located in more humble surroundings such as windmills and even living rooms, wholly dependent on donations and vol-

unteers. There are museums dedicated to just about everything: outdoor motors, waste, cigar rings, alarm clocks, matches, irons and frogs to name a few at random. The Dutch seem to have succeeded in preserving their entire heritage for the next generation.

The Dutch penchant for prudence is also reflected in another highly organised and multi-faceted circuit, where goods are collected, renovated and sold. The country has countless stores specialising in clothes, toys, music, furniture, computers, period pieces and bric-à-brac, stores that are only too keen to return to the market all those goods that the former owners finally managed to distance themselves from. These stores, often located in secret hideaways, are the least well-known tourist attraction of the Netherlands. ■

05 Private collection of Sphinx crockery, Maasticht **06** A school-class being shown around in the Teylers Museum in Haarlem **07** Museum Gaudette in Boxtel. The owner once ran a bicycle shop here. Now he collects holy figures **08** Jopie Huisman Museum in Workum. Jopie Huisman was a trader in iron and a rag-and-bone man, and also a self-educated painter. His job inspired him, as did ordinary people. He left hundreds of paintings and drawings, now exhibited in the very popular museum